THE LIFE

OF

POPE PIUS IX.

BY THE REV. ALEXIUS MILLS.

VOLUME I.

FROM 1792 TO 1868.

LONDON:

D. LANE, 310, STRAND. W.C.
1877.

LONDON:
PRINTED BY D. LANE, 310, STRAND, W.C.

TO

HIS VERY DEAR BROTHERS,

THE CLERGY OF WESTMINSTER AND SOUTHWARK,

UNWEARIED SOLDIERS IN THE BATTLE OF FAITH,
WHO IN A SHALLOW TRANSITION AND GODLESS AGE
EXHIBIT TO THE ASTONISHED EYES OF A MOCKING WORLD
THE OLD GRAND CATHOLIC LOYALTIES :
UNSWERVING FIDELITY TO HOLY CHURCH, AND A GALLANT RALLYING
ROUND THE PERSON OF THE VICAR OF CHRIST
IN THE HOUR OF EXTREME PERIL,
THE FOLLOWING PAGES ARE AFFECTIONATELY DEDICATED.

FULHAM, MARCH 1st, 1877.

PREFACE.

IN attempting to write the life of one of the greatest Pontiffs that has ever occupied the Chair of Peter, I have endeavoured to say nothing but the truth. For this reason, amongst others: I was addressing one class only. As to the rest, who prefer fiction before fact, and with whom success and material prosperity are the touch-stones of worth, they will in all probability cast these simple volumes scornfully aside. This will be perfectly *en règle*, and one of their few consistencies. One word to party-critics, and I have done: My manner I leave wholly at their mercy; my matter lies far beyond their reach.

CONTENTS.

CHAPTER I.

CHAPTER XXVIII.

THE LIFE OF POPE PIUS IX.

CHAPTER I.

The Mastai Family—The Birth of Giovanni Maria—Youthful Traits—
He Leaves Home—His First Examination.

At the beginning of the fifteenth century, a family named Mastai left Crema, in Lombardy, and came to dwell in Sinigalia, a small fortified town in the Papal Delegation of Urbino.

The members of this family were not long in acquiring position and influence in their adopted country, and at the close of the seventeenth century we find several of them ennobled, for "long and brilliant services," by the Dukes of Parma. A matrimonial alliance with the last representative of the house of Ferretti, gave to the Mastais an additional name which has been borne ever since by the sons of the family.

On the 13th of May, 1792, was born the future Pontiff Giovanni Maria Mastai Ferretti. His parents were Count Jerom and Countess Catherine Solazzi Mastai.

It is said that during the earliest years of his childhood, his pious mother was unceasing in her anxious watchfulness over the young heart of her son, and that on one.

B

occasion when remonstrated with for what appeared to be undue solicitude for one child, to the neglect of the rest, she replied in words to which after events have imparted a singular force, "Who can tell how much heroism in all virtue may be one day required of this soul."

Mastai was only seven years old, when the sufferings of the Pontiff Pius VI. caused the greatest alarm and grief in the chateau of the count, his father.

"What is the matter, Madre Mia?" asked the child, seeing his mother in tears one day.

"Ah! boy, evils long dreaded have at length fallen— armed men have taken Pius VI. prisoner; he is now in captivity far from Rome."

"Does God permit the Pope to be treated like a robber?" said the child.

"Alas, yes; the French are all powerful."

"But if we pray, Heaven will punish them," replied the child.

"We must never ask the God of Mercy for vengeance, carissime," said this Christian parent, "we will pray that the Pope's enemies may be converted."

"Madre Mia," said the child, falling upon his knees, "I will pray for Pius VI. and all his enemies."

"Had it pleased Providence," exclaims a celebrated writer, "to grant this tender child a glance into futurity —to forsee that fifty years later he himself would occupy that position in which Pius VI. suffered so much, the sight of the ingratitude which was destined to repay the noble generosity of a loving father would have crushed his tender heart."

But the members of the Mastai family had others to weep and pray for besides the Sovereign Pontiff.

The Count's brother Andrew, Bishop of Pesaro, having refused to acknowledge the French domination, endured a long and painful imprisonment in the citadel of Mantua. Indeed, the whole family suffered more or less, on account of their devotedness to the Roman Pontiff.

The day at length arrived when Giovanni Maria was to leave home for the first time.

He entered the College of the Religious called Scolpii, at Volterra, which then enjoyed a great reputation for piety and learning, and there he applied himself to his studies with the most exemplary diligence.

A few months before leaving the College, an inspector from the French University came to examine the pupils. The answers of young Mastai to the questions proposed filled all who were present with admiration. But what especially drew the inspector's attention was the modest conduct, as well as the open pleasing countenance of the distinguished pupil. After viewing him in silence for a moment, he said to the principal—

"Yonder lad is destined to do great things, if circumstances should prove at all favourable."

We are about to see how this prediction was verified.

CHAPTER II.

At the age of 18, Mastai Ferretti came to Rome to complete his studies.

The time had also arrived when it was necessary for him to choose his state of life. A religious feeling seemed to draw him towards the sanctuary, yet his health, which was feeble, presented a grave obstacle to the priesthood. For a moment his mind fixed itself upon the profession of arms, and he resolved to enter the service of the "Noble Guard."

However, God had other designs in regard to him, and, when he offered himself, he met with a refusal, on account of the weakness of his constitution.

This repulse left him in a state of painful indecision as to the future, and caused him to redouble his prayers and good works, so that he might draw down upon his perplexity light and guidance from above.

In the meanwhile, he began publicly those acts of charity by which his after life was to be so distinguished.

There lived at this time in Rome a poor but charitable workman, Giovanni Borgi.

Full of the true spirit of religion, this real Christian, when the labours of the day were over, would often pass whole nights in watching the sick, soothing their anguish by tender offices and words of charity.

. One night, returning homewards, he espied as he crossed the Piazza Rotunda, two little children lying on the steps of the Pantheon. On questioning them he found that they were orphans. This word was sufficient to procure for them a father and protector. Borgi took them to his little home. By degrees, others were brought to him, and at length the house of this good man became a real hospice for poor abandoned infants. He called them his children; they in return gave him but one name; that of "Tata Giovanni," which, in homely English, may be rendered "Daddy John."

Young Mastai was a theological student, when the rumour began to spread through Rome of the good work which a simple labouring man was doing for poor children. He desired to see Giovanni Borgi.

Old "Tata" received him in the midst of his adopted family, and related to him how God had made use of an illiterate mason to preserve those innocents from destruction.

Such earnest simplicity and devotedness could not fail to touch deeply the soul of the pious student; and from that hour the hospice of "Tata Giovanni" was taken under his protection, and the orphans of Rome found for their guardian him whom God had selected to be the Father of all the faithful.

In 1817 Mastai Ferretti received an invitation to a work most agreeable to his nature. This was to join a number of ecclesiastics who were about to give a Mission in his native town. Odescalchi and Scambi, of saintly memory, were among his companions in this labour of rescuing souls from death.

It is still remembered how, day after day, and very often during the night, the future Pontiff laboured in instruct-

ing, in admonishing, in preparing for the sacraments, many
who for years had neglected every Christian duty.

It was now that he began to feel more keenly than
ever one deep regret. He had not received Holy Orders,
and was therefore debarred from the most important
work of the missionary. To put an end to his indecision,
he sought an interview with Pius VII., who had always
shown towards him the affection of a father.

The august Pontiff listened patiently while he laid
before him his thoughts, his fears, and aspirations. At
length, speaking "like one having power,"

"Be not afraid, my son," said he, "offer yourself to
God for the work of His Church, and be assured that He
will give you health to do it."

The young Mastai received these words as an oracle.
His zeal for the divine service seemed to be re-enkindled,
and, with the advice of his confessor, he undertook a
pilgrimage to Loretto to obtain the blessing of the Mother
of God. He returned to Rome in perfect health; the
doubts regarding his vocation had left him, and he
entered more earnestly than ever upon those studies
which were to lead him to the altar of God.

There were at that time in the college many young
men of high birth, who devoted themselves to the
humblest offices of charity, in accordance with the true
Christian spirit. It was with such that the Abbate
Mastai entered into friendship, joining them in their
pious works. His visits to the hospice of Giovanni became more frequent; in fact, it was there he spent every
moment at his disposal. Need we say that to his companions he was a bright example, and to his superiors an
object of admiration?

should be taken from us, and that another should
fill his place.

No sooner had he spoken what seemed to us words of
wisdom, than the whole refectory resounded with a cry of
grief and desolation.

We threw ourselves into his arms, we knelt at his feet,
and implored him by every tender name not to abandon us.
Who would love us as he had done?

Who like him could instruct and console us? Pressing
us one by one to his bosom, while the tears streamed from
his eyes,—

"My children," said he, "I never knew until now how
much I loved you. I never thought that separation would
be so painful. If your affection for me be real, you will
show it now by obedience to my successor, by loving God
and every neighbour, by acceptance of the Heavenly Will
in every event of life."

Saying these words, he tore himself away from us and
retreated hastily to his chamber.

The sun rose brightly, ushering in another fair Italian
summer day, but over the Tata Giovanni the sky seemed
clouded.

The inmates were for a second time orphans.

The conduct of the Abbate Mastai during the legation
to Chili proved that the Sovereign Pontiff had not been
deceived in the choice he had made. Surrounded by diffi-
culties and legal complications of every kind, the young
"auditor" displayed a courage and penetration, joined with
prudence and sweetness, that he often prevailed
over the diplomacy of the corrupt Chilian authorities.

It forms part of general history how the happy
results obtained by the Court of Rome from this legation

were defeated by the machinations of those who always think it their interest to embroil the southern republics with the powers of the Church.

However, this embassy had cne effect. It made evident the character of Mastai Ferretti, for it drew into public notice those qualities and gifts which hitherto his Christian reserve had been able, in a great measure, to conceal. So that when after an absence of two years the envoys of the Holy See, worn out by disappointments, privations, and failure, turned their weary steps homewards, the name of Mastai Ferretti had gone before them, and the reputation of his talents was the topic of conversation throughout the Eternal City.

Many are the anecdotes related of Mastai Ferretti during his stay in the new world. They exhibit some of the most beautiful traits of the human character. Thus it is told how, on one occasion, he nursed with all a woman's tenderness, an English officer safely through a raging fever. Another time he remained behind his companions on the march, in order to instruct and baptize a poor heathen who lay at the point of death. He stayed beside him until he breathed his last, burying him in a grave which he dug with his own hands, and placing a humble cross of wood over the desolate spot, to tell the chance passer-by of the visitation of faith and love.

One day in passing from Valparaiso to Lima on board a small Chilian felucca, they encountered a furious tempest. The vessel was on the point of being dashed to pieces against the rocks, when a little barque, manned by some negroes, came gallantly to their rescue, headed by a fisherman named Bako. The latter jumped on board the felucca, and taking the direction of the helm, he succeeded, by his perfect knowledge of that difficult treacherous coast, in reaching at last the port of Arica.

The day after his escape from this peril, Mastai visited the poor fisherman in his hut, and, having thanked him warmly as his deliverer, placed a purse in his hands containing 400 piastres (£80), and took his leave. But the true-hearted never forget an act of kindness.

Created Supreme Pontiff, Pius IX. remembered the man who had risked his life to save him, and Bako, to his astonishment, received one day the portrait of the Pope and a handsome sum of money. The former piastres of the Abbate Mastai had, however, fructified in the hands of the fisherman, so that when the present of Pius IX. reached the little seaport of Peru it found Bako a rich man. The money was to him of little account, but the thoughtful affection and goodness of the Holy Father deeply moved him, and stirred those noble feelings which Christian generosity never fails to arouse.

There now stands a small chapel by the fisherman's hut, the cross surmounting it looks down upon the moaning sea, and, as you enter, the portrait of Pius IX. will meet your gaze. The chapel is the offering made to God by the piety of Bako, in thankful memory that he, a poor fisherman, was employed by Providence to save from death the future head of Christ's Church upon earth.

Pius VII., the friend and patron of Mastai, died in the July of 1823, and was succeeded on the Papal throne by Leo XII. The latter, however, no less than his illustrious predecessor, had a high sense of the qualities of the young "auditor," and was fully acquainted with the services he had rendered to religion during the Chilian Mission. He was received, therefore, with the greatest esteem by the

new Pontiff, who made him Canon to the Church Santa
Maria in Via Lata.

The fervent young prelate re-commenced at Rome the
kind of life he had led before his mission to the New
World.

His days were spent in preaching, in hearing con-
fessions, and in serving once more his dear orphans at Tata
Giovanni. So that whilst men who were leaders in the
political world kept their eyes upon him as one destined
in the future to rule, the people saw in him only the in-
defatigable priest, the shining example of every Christian
virtue. After a little while, Canon Mastaï was named
president of a commission appointed to undertake the
direction of the Hospice of St. Michael.* This is one of
the largest houses of charity in the world, and requires
for its successful administration qualities of the highest
order. The event, however, proved that Leo XII. was an
acute discerner of character. In less than two years,
under the rule of Canon Mastai, this vast hospice was
restored to the prosperous condition from which it had
fallen. There was no longer a dreary deficit in its
accounts; a wise and vigilant master had given to every
department of that charitable service a new impulse and
the very spirit of success.

Until the month of May, 1827, Canon Mastai was left
in peace at the institution which owes to his labour his
present thriving condition. But there was to be a change.

Providence, which had ordained him for the very
highest pinnacle of power, would make him ready for his

---

*St. Michael's covers an area of half a mlie. It is divided into four
houses—1. The asylum for old men. 2. The hospice for aged and
infirm women. 3. A professional school for young girls, and, lastly,
a vast workshop, in which parentless boys are taught a trade.

great afterwork, by putting upon him duties and dangers, responsibilities and trials. These were to be for him the preparation for those days of fierce battle when, as the true Shepherd, he was to stand dauntless in the very pathway of death, ready to give his life for his flock.

CHAPTER IV.

The archiepiscopal throne of Spoleto, being declared vacant in May 1827, Leo XII. considered that he could not confer upon his native town a greater mark of his interest and love than by appointing Abbate Mastai to the empty See. The choice of the Sovereign Pontiff was hailed with gladness by the people of Spoleto.

" This city," says a well-known writer, " will remember, with lasting gratitude, the presence amongst them, during five stormy years, of one who came to them like a blessing and protection from heaven."

Monsignor Mastai remained at Spoleto until 1832, fulfilling all the episcopal duties with a sweetness and grace which won him the affection of all hearts. But the word that was written for him in the decrees of Providence was still " Excelsior."

In the December of the same year, Pope Gregory XVI., successor of Leo, transferred him to the bishopric of Imola, a position apparently less influential than that of Spoleto, but in reality of much more importance, and one which, in the then perilous attitude of affairs, called for the presence of a ruler equally distinguished for firm wisdom as for attractive and conciliating piety. The new archbishop—bishop as he was called—fully realized in his administration the expectations of Gregory. He proved himself able to govern with success men of every variety of disposition, and to win over the most obdurate to the side of order and religion.

On the 14th of December, 1840, Mastai was elevated to the cardinalate, and received his title from SS. Peter and Marcellus. This dignity produced no change in the simple habits of the Bishop of Imola, who seemed to have but one object and one desire—to remain in the midst of the people of his diocese, and to serve them in doing the work of his divine Master. But Heaven had decreed it should be otherwise. Indeed, years before the event, the Romans themselves felt a presentiment of his coming elevation.

It happened frequently that when the pious bishop appeared in the capital of the Christian world, called thither by some inevitable duty, words such as these would be heard, muttered by the crowd: "Behold the future Pope: God will give him to us."

The early days of June, 1846, were days of grief throughout the Roman States. Gregory XVI. was no more.

The fifteen years of his reign will always be remembered for the rapid extension of the spiritual power of the Papacy. In various countries of Europe numbers of Protestants and others outside the Church were returning to the profession of the Old Faith. But in the midst of the consolation which this afforded him, the heart of the aged Pontiff was filled with anxiety in regard to the condition of his temporal power. Men with whom revolution is life, and whom no principle of honour, nor the sacredness of any oath can bind

c

were already plotting in secret those impious schemes
which have for their object the destruction of every throne
and the uprooting of Christian society. Gregory XVI.,
however, was spared the contemplation of all the horrors
which were so soon to ensue. He died before the impend-
ing crisis arrived. He was to leave it as a legacy of
sanctifying trial to his great successor.

But before we enter upon a description of the Roman
conclave, and of that one in particular which resulted in
the election of Monsignor Mastai Ferretti as Pius IX., we
shall, perhaps, be performing a task most agreeable to our
readers if we relate a few anecdotes illustrative of the
character of the noble-hearted priest whom Heaven had
destined for so much honour and suffering.

One day, a poor woman contrived to make her way into
the very apartment of Monsignor Mastai at Imola.
Throwing herself at his feet, she implored his charity.
The good bishop's purse was, as frequently happened,
without a single bajocco (one halfpenny). However,
turning to a cupboard in which he knew some plate was
put away,

"Take these," he said, giving her some of the silver
service of his table, "you can change them at the
cambiatore."

In the evening, his steward, who (although well practised, often to his annoyance, in such deeds of charity)
was ignorant of what had passed, came in the greatest
consternation to inform the bishop that there were thieves
in the palace, and that several pieces of plate were missing
from a certain cupboard. The peculiar smile that met his
statement led the faithful old servant to suspect the truth,
but the words which accompanied it left no doubt in his

mind as to the fate of the missing articles. "Do not disturb yourself, friend," said the bishop, "God has disposed of those things."

A worthy inhabitant of Imola found himself on one occasion embarrassed, being unable to procure a sum of money for which he was greatly pressed. In his difficulty, he bethought him of his bishop, then Cardinal Priest, and hastened to the palace.

"What sum do you require?" asked the Cardinal.

"Your eminence, 200 francs."

"Alas, I have not a bajocco at this moment," replied the prelate: "but stay, those candlesticks on the mantelpiece are of silver, sell them, they will, perhaps, fetch forty crowns."

The man departed joyfully with his present, leaving the cardinal to arrange how he should explain the disappearance of those things to his major-domo. He had not been long gone when another visitor was announced. This was the goldsmith, to whom had been taken the prelate's gift, and who having recognised them, had caused the man who had brought them to be arrested.

"Your Eminence has been robbed."

"Not as I am aware."

"Oh! pardon me, you have; the robber brought part of the booty for me to purchase, but I knew them instantly."

"Ah! true; those candlesticks; but they have not been stolen, and if in the least suitable to you in trade you may buy them with a safe conscience."

The love of Monsignor Mastai towards his flock was such that, on more than one occasion, it drew upon him the rebuke of those in authority. The following incident

took place after the insurrection of 1831-32, whilst he
was yet Archbishop of Spoleto :—

An agent of the Roman police had with great difficulty
obtained a list of the chief of the conspirators. Before
forwarding it, however, to Rome, he came with an air of
some consequence to show it to the archbishop. The
latter—true father of his people—had no desire to be
their judge. Taking the paper from the agent's hand, he
appeared to read it, but in reality was busy thinking how
it could be disposed of. It was winter time, and the
fire in the apartment was burning brightly. What more
natural than such an accident as was about to happen ?

" My poor child," said the archbishop, regarding the
officer with a satisfied smile, " you do not understand
your trade. When the wolf rushes down to tear the
sheep he never sends word beforehand to the shepherd."
At the same time he let fall the fatal list into the flames.

Monsignor Mastai received for this act of charity
(which defeated human justice) a sharp reprimand from
Rome. " He had committed a sort of fault," says an
eloquent writer," but it was one which saints fall into,
and indeed from which they hardly ever can restrain
themselves." Some days before the scene just related
the good archbishop had displayed Christian courage as
well as charity. The inhabitants of Spoleto had been
drawn into the insurrection which had then become
general throughout Italy.

It may be mentioned that, under the Pontificate of
Gregory XVI., whenever the slightest symptom of
disaffection appeared in any of the Roman States, it was
always the power of Austria and Austrian soldiers that
suppressed it. The detestation of Italy for the house of

Hapsburg is proverbial and natural, and she has taken care to write the proofs of her hatred in the history of modern Europe. The news had no sooner spread that Spoleto had joined the insurgents, than 2000 Austrian troops marched upon the town, and prepared to make an example of its audacity. Great was the consternation within the gates when tidings came of the approach of the enemy. The inhabitants knew well that they had little mercy to expect at the hands of this infuriated and triumphant soldiery. But what cannot the courage of love effect? With Christian dauntlessness the faithful pastor went forth alone, exposing his own life for the safety of his flock. He met the Austrian general on his way to the devoted city, and by that same power which Pope Leo used to stay the fury of Alaric he succeeded in turning the enemy aside from his revengeful purpose. Spoleto was saved from pillage and the sword.

During the days of the carnival of 1835, there was Exposition of the Blessed Sacrament in the cathedral church of Imola. Kneeling at the foot of the altar, absorbed in prayer, was to be seen the bent form of the holy bishop long after the ordinary worshippers had left the sacred building.

The evening was fast closing in, and its shadows were obscuring the most familiar objects, when suddenly, piercing shrieks for help rang through the silence of the cathedral, breaking harshly upon the contemplation of the solitary worshipper, and restoring him to thoughts of earth again. He rose from his knees and hastened towards the spot from whence the cries had proceeded.

Stretched at the foot of one of the pillars of the cathedral he perceived the body of a man, weltering in blood.

The truth flashed upon the bishop's mind in a moment; a street quarrel, a sudden stab, and then the unhappy victim had escaped from the hands of his assassins, had sought refuge in the protection of God's house, and had fallen at the sacred threshhold.

With the tenderest care did the holy prelate strive to staunch the sufferer's wounds. He was so occupied, when he saw himself confronted by three or four furious men, who, with uplifted daggers, threatened him if he interfered between them and their vengeance.

But they did not know the chivalrous heroism born from faith and love in the true priest's heart.

Springing before the helpless man at his feet, and placing his own body within reach of the assassins' weapons, "Stay," he cried, in a voice of thunder, "Will you do foul murder at the very feet of God? Having shed blood already, monsters, do you wish to drink it? This man belongs to me, this is my house, for it is God's—fall back; your presence taints the sanctuary."

Stupefied and overcome by such energy and such words, the assassins skulked away like pardoned criminals.

Left alone, the bishop renewed his charitable attentions to the wounded man, who, after a while, opened his eyes, and appeared to recover his recollection. With joyful emotion, the bishop seized the opportunity to draw from this unfortunate victim a confession of his sins. He absolved and blessed him.

When some of the attendants of the cathedral entered, soon after, they beheld a strange spectacle. It was their own bishop, kneeling by the body of the murdered man, weeping as a mother who has lost her child.

Was it extraordinary that such loving kindness won the affection of all that were good and true? that it was easily able to convert honourable opponents into the most steadfast friends?

When Monsignor Mastai was about to leave Spoleto, a deputation of the chief inhabitants went to Rome, and implored Pope Gregory not to inflict upon them so unspeakable an injury. At Imola, when the news arrived that their bishop had been elected to the supreme Pontificate, the people wept whilst they rejoiced. "It is true," they said, "the whole Church has received a blessing, but we have lost a father."

CHAPTER V.

We venture to commence this chapter with a short description of the peculiarities observed in the election of a Supreme Pontiff for Rome and for the Church.

Although it depends entirely upon the cardinals themselves in what place they will hold their conclave, the choice usually falls upon the Vatican, or its sister palace, the Quirinal. These, from their size, and their proximity to the great basilicas, are naturally marked out as most fitting for this purpose.

During the nine days' obsequies which are always observed for a deceased Pope, workmen are busy erecting, in one or other of these palaces, as many cells as there are cardinals to enter into conclave.

On the morning of the tenth day, having assisted at a Mass *de Spiritu Sancto*, these latter walk in procession to the conclave, where they remain shut up until the election of the new Pope has taken place. The great door of the hall in which the cells are built is secured with four bolts and as many locks, an aperture being left, through which the imprisoned prelates are supplied with food. The keys of the palace are consigned to the care of an ecclesiastic chosen by the cardinals themselves, who is called "Governor of the Conclave."

Each cardinal has with him a secretary, named *conclavista*, and two domestics.

Whilst the members of the Sacred College were, by a spontaneous burst of acclamation, testifying their agreement in this election, the new Pope had cast himself before the altar. Who can tell how much of solemn presentiment fell upon his soul that hour, or whether the veil hanging between his sight and the future was not partially withdrawn, so as to perfect that heroism which had already learned to say " Not my will, but Thine be done ? "

The bell of the cardinal-deacon had sounded, announcing to the prelates assembled at the doors of the Pauline Chapel that a Pope was elected. The masters of ceremonies and the secretary of the Sacred College had been admitted, and still the new Pontiff stayed on his knees at prayer. At length the cardinal sub-deacon, attended by the chief among the prelates, advanced, in order to complete all the prescribed formalities of the Pontifical election.

" Dost thou accept the choice made of thee for Supreme Pontiff ? " demanded the official.

" I accept," was the answer, given in a firm voice.

" What name will you choose to assume ? " continued the interrogator.

" That of Pius, my glorious predecessor in the See of Imola."

These acts of acceptance and nomination having been entered by the Apostolic Notary, Mastai Ferretti, now Pius IX., was arrayed in the insignia of his new dignity, and received from the Cardinal, Riario Sforza, the ring of the Fisherman. Then all present knelt, paying the first homage to the new Pope-King.

Night had already closed in, and the deepest silence

had succeeded to all the agitation of a day full of such
events as the past, when Pius IX. regained the solitude
of the cell that had been allotted to him two days before
as one of the cardinals of the conclave.

Before, however, seeking that repose which the fatigue
and emotion he had undergone demanded, he wrote to
his three brothers at Sinigaglia, to inform them of his
election :—

"It has pleased God, who exalts and who humbles, to
raise me from insignificance to the highest dignity on
earth. May His will be done. I feel the immensity of
the burden placed upon me, for I know how weak I am
to sustain it. Obtain prayers, and do you also pray for
me. Should my native city wish for some public demonstration, I beg that the whole sum collected shall
be devoted by the mayor and his officers to objects which
they shall judge to be of benefit to the people. As to
yourselves, my dear brothers, I embrace you with all my
heart in Christ Jesus. Do not be· vain of the honour
which has been put upon me. Rather pity your poor
brother, who gives you his apostolical benediction."

CHAPTER VI.

Tuesday, the 16th of June, 1846, was a gala day throughout Rome. The people, in holiday attire, crowded the great thoroughfares; every palace, every dwelling, was hung with garlands; the basilicas put on all their glory; the bells of the Eternal City rang joy peals; the thunder of the cannon from St. Angelo denoted a triumph. From the balcony of the Quirinal proclamation had been made that Mastai Ferretti, Cardinal Archbishop of Imola, had been exalted to the pontifical throne, with the title of Pius IX. Not only Rome, but the whole of Italy, except the Austrian faction, was transported with joy at the tidings. As the news of his election spread throughout Europe, it was received everywhere with a satisfaction which was soon after to grow into a perfect enthusiasm.

The new Pontiff commenced his reign with an act which, whatever may be thought of its policy, was at all events gracious. A general amnesty for past offences was granted. Political delinquents were set at liberty; the refugees were recalled, on condition of their giving a solemn pledge for their future conduct. The reader will, perhaps, be interested if we give the words of the preamble to this act of noble-hearted policy:—" In these days, when our heart is moved to see public joy manifested at our being raised to the pontificate, we cannot refrain from a feeling of grief in thinking that a certain number of families are unable to participate in the common joy because they bear the pain of some offences committed by some of their members against society and the sacred rights of the legitimate prince. We, therefore, etc."

The words of the oath taken by the released and pardoned Revolutionist were as follows:—"I pledge myself, on my word of honour, not to abuse, in any way or at any time, this act of sovereign clemency."

Many of them added of their own accord these words:— "I swear to shed my blood in defence of Pius IX.; I renounce my share of Paradise if I betray the oath of honour that binds me to him."

It speaks badly for that party known at the present day as "Young Italy," that in less than two years they whom the Sovereign Pontiff had restored to their country, violated, almost to a man, their solemn oaths, and, in fact, headed the revolution which sent their too merciful prince into exile. Indeed, it is now proved beyond all doubt that these men had scarcely entered Rome before they began, once more, their insensate traitorous plots.

Two days after the amnesty to the political offenders, the Pontiff set free the unhappy men confined in the Roman prisons for debt. This act of clemency roused the spirit of generous emulation in many of the chief citizens, who commenced subscription lists for the relief of these unfortunates, for whom a considerable sum was realized.

"The people, your Holiness," said Ventura, "read in this act your determination that, whilst you live, no

Roman shall be imprisoned unjustly." "If they read
this," replied the Pope, "they read aright; for such a
resolve is written upon my heart."

The work of reasonable liberty and consistent progress
was not allowed to stand still. Every reform which the
happiness of his people seemed to require was undertaken
at once and carried out with energy. The tribunals were
remodelled, a new commercial tariff was published, by
which the import duties on many articles of consumption
were reduced, and a great source of corruption, viz., the
granting of patents, was altogether abolished. A National
Junta was created, as well as the Municipal Council and
the Civic Guard. The civil and criminal codes were
revised, order was re-established in the finances, and new
councillors, more acceptable to the nation, were appointed.
Prelates, in the name of the Pope, went through the
States of the Church, to hear the complaints of the people;
while he himself, remembering his former work of love at
the "Tata Giovanni" and the Hospice of St. Michael,
devoted all he could spare from his slender resources to
the erection of houses of charity and schools for orphans.

In the meanwhile he published the fundamental
statute of a representative government, restored the public
audiences, and granted the press a tolerance unheard of
at that time through the whole Peninsula, and not known
at the present day in enlightened France. With his own
eyes he scrutinized the management of hospitals and
prisons; by his order and under his superintendence
public works were commenced, railway companies obtained
the most generous concessions, and gas was introduced
into the public thoroughfares.

The Italian people were in a delirium of joy. Through

D

out the provinces of the Papal States it was one succession
of fêtes.   The rejoicings for the accession of Mastai
Ferretti to the Pontifical throne lasted a whole year.
The good Pope loved to appear in the streets of his
capital not so much as monarch as a fond father. Plainly
dressed, he was to be seen walking through the streets of
Rome, visiting the sick, attending the schools, and followed everywhere by the blessings and the prayers of
devoted thousands.

"Pius IX.," says one who has always been his enemy,
"has a heart and a confidence which nothing can daunt;
his face beams with the calm of a good conscience."

An illustrious traveller in Italy in 1847, after an
audience at the Vatican, wrote, "I have at last seen the
new Pope ; he is grace, dignity, and sweetness combined.
I only echo the public sentiment when I tell you that
he is adored here."

" Born to be a king ! " was the exclamation of a prince,
referring to Pius IX.

The young Protestant Princess of Prussia, after a short
interview at St. Peter's, said, "My heart is full; I have
enjoyed the happiness of seeing and hearing Pius IX."

A correspondent of a London paper wrote : " One can
form no idea of the emotion of the people here, and the
joy that lights up their faces, when the Pope appears [in
public."

" The Romans for the time had but one cry : "Long
live the good Pius IX. ! Long live the father of his
people ! "

The same spirit animated every village and town of the
Patrimony.   Crowds waited upon his carriage, and
surrounded him when on foot.   At his return on one

CHAPTER VII.

The Revolutionists and the "Retrogradists"—The Enemies of the New Measures—The Replies of Pius IX. to Austria, &c.—His Firmness in Removing Abuses—The Envoy of the Sultan at the Vatican—Ineffectual Remonstrance of France—The Famine in Ireland and Pius IX.

While the chief of the Catholic world was thus engaged in ameliorating the condition of his people, there were thoughtful men, deeply versed in political wisdom, who, looking around them, saw enough even then to create alarm and suspicion.

They beheld among the crowds who followed the footsteps of the Pontiff with shouts and vivas those who had only one design and one vow—to urge on the Government to pass the barriers of prudence, so that the work of socialism and revolution might be effected under the disguise and protection of legitimate reform.

We shall see in its proper place how true was that instinct which warned of the coming danger even when all seemed calm and still. But whatever may be public opinion regarding the expediency of some of the measures adopted in the fulness of his generosity by Pius IX., only one judgment can be passed upon his enemies. These were of two parties—the Revolutionists, whose leading doctrines were (and still are) "no property" (except for themselves), "no religion, and no family ties," and who hoped to profit by the Pope's concessions, so as to overthrow society; and, secondly, "those of his own household," many of the cardinals and prelates in the interest of Austria and France, "Retrogradists" and domestic traitors, more to be dreaded than any open foe. Thus the two extremes of society—revolution and absolutism— if they did not unite for the time, laboured at least for the same end, viz., to defeat the noble work of the great leader of Italian liberty.

The consequence of this treason will be apparent as we advance in our task, but it can be summed up here in one sentence—the betrayal of Charles Albert and of Pius IX,. and the ruin of Italian independence.

It soon became apparent that the Roman Pontiff was to be left to fight the battle of true constitutional liberty alone. Friends fell away from him on every side. Austria, Russia, France, Prussia, and even England, addressed to him notes of warning and reproof. The Genius of Freedom, aroused from the slumber of exhaustion, had startled them. Lutzow, the Austrian ambassador, added threats to remonstrances, and advised his Cabinet to a movement of troops along the frontier.

At Pesaro, Urbino, and other towns, injurious placards were affixed to the walls by the same agency, whilst, by means of its adherents in the Sacred College, and by encouraging the rage of displaced *employées*, Austria succeeded in exciting against the Pontiff a perfect hierarchy of those who had lived·upon the abuses which he reformed.

But it was all labour in vain. No amount of opposition made Pius IX. hesitate one instant. To every representation the answer was at once dignified and hopeless. To Naples, who complained of his granting freedom to the press, he replied, " When I look into the annals, I find the King of Naples is vassal to the Pope of Rome ; your

suzerain does not receive your dictation." To the
Austrian ambassador, who said, " We hear nothing now
spoken of but Italian union and Italian independence,"
he answered, "These phrases were old before I was born ;
they will be heard of after us ; and, as an Italian, I
confess they have my sympathy."

The remonstrance of France, which was also directed
against the liberty granted to the press in the Papal
States, was silenced with these cutting words : " Tell the
King of France that I do not remember ever interfering
with the Parisian journals." " Ce Pape me perdra,"
exclaimed old Louis Philippe, in very despair.

When told that many of the newspapers accused him
of introducing all his reforms from the vulgar motive of .
seeking popularity, "Ah," he said, " they will know one
day all my motives ; but, whether popular or not, I shall
do my duty. This, however, is certain, I shall never
deceive the people who have honoured me."

The same firmness which he exhibited in his inter-
course with foreign Courts characterized his conduct
at home. It was the prelude to the celebrated " Non
possumus," which was afterwards to throw into
mortal agonies the crafty diplomacy of Piedmont and
France.

When he desired to establish the National Guard, the
Council of State voted to a man against it. The scrutiny
of the urn revealed nothing but black balls—a result very
significative of the determination of the members. Taking
off his white calotte, the Pope placed it over the votes.
" See, gentlemen," he said, " we can change the colour of
these things." Need it be added that the obnoxious
Guard was at once organized ? At the introduction by

Pius of a more efficient police for the streets of Rome, many complaints, as might have been expected, were heard from those who suffered by this change from bad to good. Amongst others, there was a nobleman (?) who presented himself on one occasion before the Pontiff with a grievance for which he sought redress. The police had removed from the front of his palace certain hucksters, who, from time immemorial, had been the nuisance of the neighbourhood, besides impeding the footway with their different wares.

"What do these people pay you for the privilege you grant them?" asked the Pope.

"Holy Father, 3000 crowns a year."

"And for a long time?"

"Since 1791, your Holiness, this sum has been received by our family."

"Three thousand crowns," replied the Pope, "and for fifty-six years 168,000 crowns—a great sum! Let me advise you, my friend, to be wise, and hold your peace. This pathway, which you and your family have obstructed for so long a time, belongs to the municipality. Should they hear to what good account you have turned their property, they would certainly commence an action for restitution. Say, therefore, no more about it; as for me, you may rely on my discretion."

On another occasion, when he suspected that corruption was at work with regard to a vacant canonry, taking up the list of applicants, and regarding it for a moment, he exclaimed, "The name of the man who deserves it is not here; I mean the Abbate Ponzilene, a hard-working, good priest; him I appoint."

The movement occasioned all through Italy by the

progressive policy of the Pontifical Court produced the greatest uneasiness in Vienna, always in a panic for the security of its Lombardo-Venetian kingdom. This feeling was not allayed by an event which now took place.

The descendant of Mahomed II., the Sultan of Turkey, hearing of the virtues and the wisdom of the Sovereign Pontiff, and desirous of arranging the vexed Eastern Question, sent an ambassador to the Court of Rome.

Since the days of Bajazet and Innocent VIII. no such envoy had set foot on Italian soil. This was one of those revolutions of which we find examples in history, but without an explanation. The successor of Urban II., who preached the first crusade, and of Pius V., prime mover of the union of all Christendom against the Turks, was to be seen in the Quirinal Palace, engaged in most friendly conference with Che Kib-Effendi, the imperial envoy, discussing the interests of Christianity in the Ottoman empire. Equally strange was the spectacle of a Mussulman, said to be devoted to his fanaticism, wearing publicly around his neck, and exhibiting as an honour, the portrait of Pius IX.

The embassy was a perfect success, and resulted in the appointment of Monsignor Valergo, former missionary in Persia, to the Latin Patriarchate of Jerusalem, with the right and obligation of residence. Thus, at the formal demand of the Ottoman Government, a natural protector of the Catholic interest was established in the East, with civil jurisdiction over the faithful, to be ever on the spot, and empowered to plead their rights before the Divan itself.

This perfect revolution in the secular tradition of European diplomacy in the East was not, however, effected without opposition. Supported by Russia and

Austria, France presented, through Count Rossi, the following protest :—

"That the right which the Sublime Porte pretends to concede to the Holy Father was exclusively reserved to France by the most ancient deeds. France has paid for them with the blood of her soldiers. It is part of her history, and one of her national glories, which she cannot at any price abandon."

The reply made to this protest by the Roman Court was brief and to the point :—" The previous arrangement with France" (it stated) "had been destroyed in 1840. The separation of the Druses and Maronites proved that the French Cabinet had no longer any power in the East."

The English ministry, glad of an opportunity such as before had served their purpose at Damascus, sided with the Sovereign Pontiff. Thus, men beheld the head of the Catholic religion, on a question purely relating to the interests of Catholicity, opposed by two orthodox powers, and supported by heretical England and an infidel Sultan.

And here, before closing this chapter, it will be in place to record one of the noble actions with which it may be said Pius IX. concluded the few happy days of his long and sorrowful Pontificate. He is King of Rome always, but he is more; he is spiritual lord of the whole earth besides. The sufferings of his children in any part of the world are sure to receive from him sympathy and help.

A little while after he ascended the throne, the dreadful destroying angel of famine appeared in Ireland. The history of this scourge is to be found elsewhere. Suffice it to say, that while the caitiff Whigs in this country delayed and delayed, and argued and wrangled about the "rights of trade" being respected, &c., myriads of the people perished amidst all the horrors of starvation and fever. The population of the "sister" kingdom was reduced by two millions. How did Pius IX. act? In a letter addressed to the whole Catholic world he wrote thus: "I urge you to run to the relief of this famine. What great efforts ought we not especially to make, when we remember how constant the fidelity of the clergy and the people of Ireland is, and always has been, to the Apostolic See?" His own offering in money and presents was 12,000 crowns.

The soil of Ireland has not grown ingratitude; twice since have the enemies of the peace of Europe found in their path that "Brigade" whose loyalty the gold of Turin was powerless to corrupt. It will need a sharper, truer sword than that which Piedmont wears to cut away the defences that faith and love will again raise to restore the throne to the successor of St. Peter.

CHAPTER VIII.

The condition of Italy when Pius IX. ascended the Pontifical throne was such that a far less liberal policy than that which he displayed would have been sufficient to have rekindled the hopes alike of good and bad amongst the Italian populations. The Duke of Modena had been restored, and ruled with an iron hand. In Parma discontent was rife, notwithstanding the gentle government of Maria Louisa. In Sardinia, Charles Albert had changed the mild administration which had marked the commencement of his reign. The people of the different States were in a condition of apparent tranquillity, the real feeling being one of general dissatisfaction, which was strengthened by the industry of the exiles and emigrants. The attempts at revolt in the Romagna in 1843 and 1844, and the insurrection at Rimini in 1845, were signs not to be mistaken of the ferment that was working underneath. Along with these revolutionary tendencies, there existed also, in the minds of the orderly and educated, a definite wish to procure a moderate amount of reform. The idea of a national confederacy, a sort of Italian customs-union, or Zollverine, had long been enter-

tained, and discussed in the assemblies of the *literati*, and
seemed, indeed, to be the most feasible plan of any. In
the meantime an unaccountable languor and inaction had
crept into the Austrian Government, so that it neglected
to secure the means of energetically withstanding a
violent outbreak.

This was the state of the Peninsula when Pius IX.
was elected.

He came harmoniously, with the growing conscious-
ness of natural and political rights. His reforming
measures created, as we have seen, a sensation through
all Italy, and even beyond the Po. The new political
system of the Pontiff carried the day, and the inhabitants
of the different States whose princes had been wise
enough to imitate the policy of the head of the Church,
hailed with enthusiasm the altered times as the commencement of a new era.

They, and all Europe, were doomed to a bitter disappointment. In order to explain this clearly, our
readers must permit us a short digression.

There has been but one cause, one power, that was
able to produce all the revolutions which this century
has beheld—the power of the secret societies of Europe.
Their object is one: it is to unite together noble and
tradesman, prince and peasant, all who are willing to
bind themselves by impious oaths to labour with an
unholy patience for an unholy end. Their motto is, " No
King! no Government! no Church! no God! death to
Christ! hurrah for Hell and assassination!" Their
doctrines are a mixture of the Communism of the Cantons
with the Pantheism of Germany. The strongest argument found in their reasoning is the dagger of one of

their bravos.   He who once gives himself to this society
of lost men, is theirs, body and soul, irrevocably.   Death
is the penalty decreed for desertion, or for revealing their
secrets, or for disobedience to orders.

The Forty-sixth Article of the " Secret Code of Young
Italy " commands, that any victim who shall be marked
out for destruction shall be followed, go where he may,
and shall be slain, even though found "on the bosom of
his mother, or in the tabernacle of Christ."   Lest we
should be thought to exaggerate in our detestation of
this hideous alliance, we give an extract from a letter
found upon one of the Roman conspirators.   Amongst
other details are the following :—.

" It is of vital importance to make ourselves masters of
the Duke of Modena. . . . . As to Charles Albert, we
should seek some favourable opportunity to poignard
him.   I recommend the same course in regard to the
King of Naples. . . . . The Lombards may second our
efforts by poison, or by insurrection, under the form of
little *Sicilian Vespers*, against the Germans . . . . func-
tionaries, or private citizens, who show a hostile spirit,
must be put to death, and the report can be circulated
that they have absconded. . . . . *We must adopt any
expedient to accomplish our end.*   This is the doctrine of
our master, Machiavelli—self-interest, knavery, treason."

At the head of this unholy alliance, chief apostle of all
modern insurrections, stood Joseph Mazzini.   Born of
virtuous parents, and trained in his youth in all piety, it
was the fate of this unhappy man to fall at an early period
under the power of the leaders of the " Carbonari."
In their hands he became the enemy of every right,
human and divine.   Wherever there has been a modern

conspiracy against society, Mazzini has been its foster-
father. A fugitive from his native land, he found an
asylum in England, where a strange hospitality is always
extended to those who seek our shores, for the purpose of
plotting in safety against the thrones of the rest of
Christendom. The *Times*, of July, 1857, well describes
the particular characteristic of this disturber of the peace
of the world. It is neither complimentary nor heroic :—
"Mazzini is an incendiary, whose murderous designs
expand in proportion to his own sense of security, but
who has no such regard for the safety of his dupes. He
says to his followers, 'Go and throw yourselves into the
midst of danger and death, and I will stay safely here
and arrange fresh plots for you.'" Applying to Mazzini
the words of the gifted, but unfortunate Emmett, we
may say, "If all the blood for whose shedding he is
responsible were collected into one receptacle, this man
might swim in it." It was Mazzini who, casting
his evil eye upon the happy Rome of 1847, vowed
its destruction under the title of the "Regeneration of
Italy." He held a secret convention in Paris, in the
spring of 1847, in which Rome was determined upon as
the head-quarters of the conspiracy against all the States
of the Peninsula. "Revolution in Rome," said Mazzini to
his followers, "will make all Europe tremble." And
this was the plan of action which he sketched out :—
The Cardinals were to be denounced as enemies to the
Sovereign Pontiff, and as being completely opposed to
his administrative reforms. Public banquets were to be
held, and processions and gatherings of the people in the
streets encouraged, for this would accustom the masses
to assemble quickly, and would teach them to feel their

E

strength. The speeches and the songs upon these occa-
sions were to be moderate at first, extolling the glories
of "Italy united," and proclaiming the idea of an "ever-
lasting Italian confederation." Demand after demand
was to be made upon the Pontiff; sweeping changes,
which it was known he could never grant, were to be
called for, and the first refusal was to be the signal for
disturbance and outbreak; and the revolution once commenced was to be named a "religious and a sacred war,"
undertaken merely to expel the Austrians. Such a title
would win over even those who were most closely attached
to the Pope.

Such was the programme presented to the conspirators
by their leader in the spring of 1847.

We sincerely hope that the patience of the reader has
not been too severely tried by us, the digression into
which we have ventured seemed essential to the perfect
understanding of many a future chapter. Now we
return.

We have seen elsewhere how Austria in particular had
protested against the policy inaugurated by the Sovereign
Pontiff, and how, in fact, she had menaced him with
intervention. In her remonstrances she had been joined
by France and Naples, which States, however, contented
themselves with mere angry protests. Not so the Court
of Vienna. In every State of the "Patrimony" its
agents were at work endeavouring to agitate the people.
At Bologna the proclamations set up by the Pontifical
Government were covered with mud. Determined, no
matter in what way, to effect their purpose, they went
so far as to adopt for a time almost the revolutionary
argument, and endeavoured to exasperate the different

populations by circulars and pamphlets, in which it was
asserted that the Pope was granting all these reforms for
a time only. Their nefarious schemes were not altogether unsuccessful. A liberal distribution of money
had already gained over to their side the lowest of the
rabble, some ex-police, and a few soldiers. In fact, the
Cabinet of Vienna in its panic was ready to grasp at any
pretext for marching an armed force south of the Po.
As such did not present itself, it was resolved to try and
create it. Already the princes of Italy had been gained
over to its side, by the insinuation that there was on foot
a confederation against them, headed by the Pope and
Charles Albert.

In defence of the conduct of Austria, it has been urged
that her hostility was directed solely against the Revolutionists, whose ulterior designs she was able to read.
This may be so ; yet it will be always true that whatever
her object, she plotted against the Pontiff in a manner
unintelligible in a Catholic power, and that she violated
(as we shall see later) the conditions of the Treaty of
Vienna for no conceivable purpose, except to stay the
progress of the enthusiasm which Pius IX. had enkindled.
It cannot be denied, also, that in 1847 a man who had
been watched for some weeks as a spy was seized by the
Roman police, and that upon him were found documents
clearly proving that Austria was deeply implicated in
some scheme to seize the person of the Pope. Pius IX.
sent at once for the Austrian Ambassador and addressed
him in these words : "You condescend to plot. Write
to your sovereign, and tell him that if he expects to
intimidate me, he will find himself greatly mistaken."

The Roman people, as yet uncorrupted by the Mazzinian

emissaries, gave the same functionary a very significant
hint of their view of the conduct of the Cabinet which he
represented.   In the midst of the illuminations and wild
merriment of one of the evenings of the Carnival of 1847,
the news spread among the crowds that the carriage of
the Austrian Ambassador was coming along the Corso.
In an instant every lamp was extinguished, the people
disappeared in silence, and the representative of a hated
Government found himself alone in the streets, which
were deserted and in darkness.

In the meanwhile, however, they who had deeply studied
the nature of revolutionary movements, and who had been
taught by bitter experience the hollowness of popular
demonstrations, saw enough already to excite just alarm.
The triumphal processions, the continual assembling of
the people, the impassioned discourses, the Hosannas in
honour of Pius IX., might these not be mere disguises
behind which the enemy was fatally at work?   At all
events, it was impossible to say at what hour the popular
exultation might not compromise public tranquillity,
especially with so feverish a people as the Italians.   In
fact, there was the greatest danger of enthusiasm
degenerating into excess.   No edict could be published
but within a quarter of an hour of its appearance all the
banners of Italy were to be seen floating before the
Quirinal.   Every day witnessed processions of the people,
to the sound of military music.   The streets were con-
tinually thronged by excited multitudes, singing the
Italian "Marseillaise," firing muskets, and shouting,
"Viva il Papa!"

It was absolutely necessary to put an end to this
exaggerated state of things, and a proclamation was

therefore issued by the Government entreating the people
to return to the quiet of their homes, and to resume their
ordinary avocations.

A request at once so natural and just, was seized upon
by the enemies of order as a means of arousing the
popular discontent and suspicion. The proclamation was
stigmatized as the work of the enemies of Italy ; the bad
advisers of the Holy Father ; and the journals, day by day,
in inflammatory language, called upon the people to run
to the deliverance of the Pontiff, who they said was being
forced by others to break his faith with the nation.

The revolutionary mask was beginning to fall. But it
was too soon for the enemies of human society to show
themselves as they really are. It was necessary first of
all to arouse the passions and blind the judgment.   Men
do not willingly love self-destruction, and the Romans in
possession of liberty, which is the legitimate daughter of
Heaven, were not as yet so corrupted as to prefer licen-
tiousness, which is the illegitimate daughter of liberty.

But now a great day was near at hand, the 17th of
July, the anniversary of the release of the political
prisoners by Pius IX. It was determined by the Romans
to make this the occasion of a great demonstration in
honour of their beloved prince and Father.

A grand pic-nic was to be given at the Torre di Guinto.
the farm of Cincinnatus (he who passed from the plough
to the dictatorship), and four thousand people had given
in their names as guests, and Cicerovacchio was the
appointed chairman.*

---

* This man, whose real name was Angelo Brunetti, was for years
a popular leader of the lower classes in Rome. Of gigantic stature
and herculean strength, and gifted with a rough, ready eloquence, he

To the astonishment of all Rome, a few days before the fêtes, a notification appeared on the walls of the city, signed by the Minister of State, announcing that the public rejoicings would be adjourned.

While men were wondering what this could mean they heard the publication of an edict commanding the instant organization of the civic guard. At the same time the citizens were summoned to the Castle of St. Angelo, where they received arms, and each man twenty-four rounds of ammunition. All this was too intelligible to be mistaken. The word secret conspiracy flew from one end of the city to the other, and roused the loyalty of the people to the highest pitch. They were right.

The Pontifical Government had received information of a desperate plot entered into for its overthrow. The plan of the conspirators had been to occupy the Corso, the Strada di Ripetti, and del Babbuino. A few hundred miscreants were to pick a quarrel with the people during the excitement of the rejoicings, which would serve as a pretext for a general onslaught, in the confusion of which the government would be paralyzed, and the person of the Pope might be secured.

Such was the conspiracy of the 17th July, 1847, which was certainly encouraged if not originated by Austria, acting in concert with domestic traitors. But the vigilance of the Pontiff stifled it in its birth.

Secure as yet in the love of his people, Pius IX. did

naturally held sway over those of his own in rank in life. At first the most devoted of the adorers of Pius IX., he afterwards fell into the snares of the Revolutionists, who wanted such a man and his followers for their deeds of violence. In their hands he became a monster of ferocity, and chief of the sacrilegious bandits who pillaged the Eternal City. He has since died in exile.

not fear to trust them with the guardianship of the city and of his own person.   Ten thousand men from the upper and middle classes gathered at his word.   The fourteen districts into which Rome is divided were sentinelled by workmen, whom the enthusiasm of the hour had transformed into citizen soldiers.

Rome was saved and Austria checkmated.

Colonel Freddi, the appointed leader of the conspirators, was lucky enough to save himself by flight.   The Governor of Rome, Grassellini, an abettor of the traitors, received the following too merciful sentence—

"Two hours are accorded to the Abbate Grassellini to quit the 'States of the Church.'"

Cardinal Minardi, an Austrian spy, was tracked by a thousand of the furious people from six in the evening till midnight.   He would have been torn into pieces but for the eloquence of the celebrated Ventura, who, with tears in his eyes, begged the Cardinal's life from the hands of his indignant captors.

Not yet Guiseppi Mazzini, not yet!

CHAPTER IX.

An important event took place at this time, which went far to prove the complicity of Austria in the plot of July, 1847.

On the allegation that a certain Captain Tanowick had been insulted by one of the people of Ferrara, the Austrian garrison received orders from the Cabinet of Vienna to take military possession of the town.

What naturally increases the suspicion that Austria was a party in the insurrection that was suppressed at Rome, is the singular fact that the disturbance in the city and the order issued regarding the occupation of Ferrara bear the same date. The latter was evidently part of the plot, or at the least, it was an unmistakable declaration on the part of Austria against the policy inaugurated by the Sovereign Pontiff.

By the 103rd article of the protocol of the Treaty of Vienna of 1815 Austria, in spite of the protest of Cardinal Consalvi, had the privilege conceded to her of a garrison in the towns of Ferrara and Commachio ; but it was distinctly stated that this gave her no right over the towns themselves.

Notwithstanding this, in defiance of all justice, and

relying on her military superiority, Austria ventured upon the dangerous experiment of enforcing her own policy, at the imminent risk of arousing the national susceptibilities of the whole Italian Peninsula.

At first indeed she proceeded with a certain amount of caution. The garrison was gradually increased. Next an Austrian major, accompanied by a picket of cavalry, made his appearance, stating that by order of his Government some troops were about to execute a few manœuvres in the interior of the city, and he requested the Governor, Cardinal Ciacchi, to issue a proclamation that might keep the people tranquil. The answer of the Cardinal proved that he was worthy of the charge committed to him.—

"I will not," he replied, "deceive my people. The consequences of this act of violence I leave to your own Government."

It was then that Austria threw off the mask.

On the 13th of August, with colours flying, Count d'Aresperg, in command of a division of the Austrian army, occupied all the important points of the city. By this act of aggression he superseded the authority of the Pontifical Government.

It was not to be expected, however, that such a violation of civil rights would be submitted to tamely.

Ciacchi, who was legate of the whole province, uttered the following dignified protest:

"I declare this act of Austria completely illegal, and contrary to the stipulations of the Treaty of Vienna. As representative of the Sovereignty of the Holy See, as Legate-Apostolic and Governor of this city and province, I protest against this and any other act of the same nature. The accident to Captain Tanowick is not proved; if it were, it can give no right to the Austrian forces to assume control in this city."

This protest was followed by another more energetic, and at the same time the Sovereign Pontiff issued a declaration approving of the remonstrance of the Cardinal and calling upon Austria to withdraw her troops from the Pontifical territory.

It was in vain that the Ambassadors of France and Vienna strove to explain away the object of this illegal seizure of the dominions of a friendly sovereign. Pius IX. was immovable in his resolution. He exhibited the sublime of moral power, and to every offer of mediation he gave but one answer :—

"Only the completest satisfaction will atone for this outrage, and the only satisfaction I will accept is instant evacuation."

In the meanwhile nothing could exceed the enthusiasm of the Italian people at the tidings of this aggression on the part of Austria. It roused all the old hatred for the traditional foe, which had never died, but had been sleeping. The whole Peninsula rose like one man.

In Bologna, in Modena, in Sicily, Calabria, and the Abruzzi, the most indescribable excitement prevailed. In the palace, in the wine shop, in the theatres, at the church doors, it was the one engrossing subject. Lists of subscriptions for the national defence no sooner appeared, than they were covered with names. The youth of Bologna declared themselves in readiness to march at once to the relief of Ferrara. Charles Albert published a protest against the conduct of the Government of Vienna, of which he sent a copy to every Court of Europe.

Poor people! for the moment they forgot that they were modern Italians, and half believed the forsworn soldier-monk when he cried out, "Ye sons of heroes of the blood of Troy, every one of you is worth a thousand of the enemy!"

From the Coliseum the crowd poured into the streets, bearing the standards of the Roman volunteers, which they carried to the palace, calling upon the Pontiff to come forth and bless them.

In answer to their repeated and furious cries, the Pope made his appearance in the balcony of the Quirinal, and uttered these memorable words : " As minister of the God of peace, I ought not to bless the torch which will set the whole of Europe in conflagration. I am at war with no one, all Christians are my children, and I press them all paternally to my heart." Then raising his hands to Heaven, he gave his benediction to Italy, and concluded by saying, " the Roman volunteers are at liberty to join the troops sent to guard the Pontifical States, but, on no account, must they cross the borders."

Such words were spoken too late, for his own subjects had already involved him in the general outburst against . Austria.

It happened that some volunteers who had joined the soldiers sent to occupy and defend Ferrara had deserted their ranks to enter the army of Charles Albert. One of them, Signor Caffi, an artist of some celebrity, was found by his companions hanging on a tree near Ferrara, with this inscription appended to his lifeless corpse: "This is the way in which the crusaders of Pius IX. are treated."

Such ruthless violation of the laws of civilized warfare on the part of the soldiers of Radetzky raised the fury of the people to a pitch that nothing could control. But this was not all.

At the review of the volunteers, General Durando compromised his Sovereign in the most unpardonable manner. "Soldiers," he said, "we have been blessed by the hand of the great Pontiff, Pius IX. He has blessed your swords, united to those of Charles Albert." And again, at Bologna, the first act of the same officer was to issue a proclamation, in which he gave the authority of the Pope as a sanction for the war.

It was this disobedience of his own troops, in entering the Venetian territory contrary to orders, and making war upon Austria of their own account, that was the occasion of many of the disasters that afterwards ensued.

The conscientious resistance which he so firmly made to the war party gave the revolutionists the finest opportunity for making Pius IX. unpopular with his subjects. In fact, the disaffection of the Roman people dates from the Encyclical of April 29th, 1848, in which the Pontiff defended his conduct to Europe.

In this noble document, after showing that he had only obeyed the instincts of the Papacy in giving rational freedom to his people, and that he had no desire to extend the Pontifical States beyond the limits fixed by Providence, he declares that his orders to his troops were that they should not pass the Papal frontier :—" Father of all the faithful, as such, we refuse to take part in the general bloodshed. It being the desire of some that we should join in the war against the Austrians, we believe it to be at length our duty to declare that it is most foreign to our counsels. . . . In accordance with the duty of our apostleship, we embrace equally with our paternal

The refusal with which these insolent demands were met was the signal for the beginning of the reign of terror in Rome. The Pontifical colours were torn down, the houses of the wealthy broken into and plundered, and the banks were pillaged of their treasury. The Roman populace, joined by the disbanded soldiers of the army of Italy, thronged the thoroughfares, crying, "Death to the cardinals!—death to the priests!" and at last the cry was, "Death to St. Peter!"

"Pius IX. cannot save Italy," said Fiorentini; "we must save ourselves without him."

CHAPTER XI.

For ten centuries there has not been an Italian so Italian as the Sovereign Pontiff.

But for him Italy would have sunk into a mere German province long since. Historical science has already avenged the memory of those high priests of Christendom who, in the middle ages, combated the very doctrines which modern revolution advocates. "The Popes," says John van Muller (called the prince of modern historians), " resisted the emperors, for the interests of the Church and in behalf of princes and people. The triumph of the Pope was always an assurance of general liberty. Humanity will one day confess that in condemning revolutionary ideas the Popes have saved the world."*

"The Papacy," says Ancillon, "stayed the despotism of the emperors ; a second Tiberius was impossible, Rome would have crushed him." " Without the Papacy, Europe would have fallen into one or more Caliphates, and have been shamefully reduced to Oriental slavery and effeminacy."†

But are we not rather simple to expect from the adversaries of the Pontifical royalty much history or political science ? The Roman anarchists soon proved

* *Hist. des Suisses.*　　　　　† Coqueril, *Hist. of Christendom.*

He entered his carriage together with Righetti, the financial representative, and drove for the Chamber of Deputies. As he approached his destination, he perceived that the Carabineers had been removed, and that in their place, contrary to orders, two battalions of the Civic Guard occupied the Piazza and Court of the Chancery. He felt at once that he was betrayed. A furious and agitated crowd was in possession of the peristyle and staircase of the building, and greeted his arrival with a storm of groans and hisses; but with a proud compassion he only smiled upon them as he alighted, and with flashing eye and form erect passed on.

The conspirators instantly closed round him, and as he pressed forward, one of them, by preconcerted signal, struck him on the shoulder with a cane. Turning fiercely to seize his aggressor, he received a mortal stab in the neck. His life-blood drenched the marble stairs of the hall to which he came to plead the cause of constitutional liberty and civil order. He perished in the very sight of two hundred pretended representatives of peaceful justice, who stretched out not a finger to prevent this crime!

This assassination of his Prime Minister was the grateful return made by the Roman people to their Sovereign for the generous amnesty with which he commenced his reign. It more than sufficed to throw them back in civilization half a century, and to remove from them the good-will of every Christian community.

Rossi perished because his courage and wisdom would have defeated the whole programme of Mazzini.

"He has died a martyr," said Pius IX., when the terrible news was conveyed to him; "God will receive his soul."

G

Young Rossi, in a frenzy of grief, rushed through the streets of Rome with his sword drawn, calling upon his father's murderer to dare to make himself known. In the piazza of the Chancery, confronting the Civic Guard, of which he was lieutenant, "Cowards!" he exclaimed, "you have dishonoured this uniform. I swear never to disgrace my manhood by wearing it again."

The revolutionists, however, gloried in their bloody deed, and under the direction of the leaders of the Clubs the mob prowled through the streets, indulging in every outrage in honour of the success which their future tyrants had achieved. And in the evening the chief murderer of Rossi, brandishing his knife in the air, was carried by torchlight upon the shoulders of his fellow-assassins down the Corso, and sang beneath the very windows of her whom that day he had made a widow.*

The glory of "Young Italy" was advancing towards its perfection.

---

* It is satisfactory to know that few of these murderers have escaped human justice. Constantini was beheaded in 1864, on the Piazza di Cerchi; Grandini, condemned to the galleys, hanged himself in prison in 1853. The rest of these miscreants, if still alive, are begging their bread in London, Berlin, and Paris.

From the morning of the attack on the Quirinal the members of the diplomatic body had been unanimous in advising the Pontiff to retire secretly from the States of the Church for a time, but he had hitherto resisted all their entreaties. "My departure," he said, "will be the signal perhaps for a sacrilegious outburst in which every monument of religion may perish." Hearing, however, that the conspirators intended to march upon the palace, and compel him to resign the temporal power, and if he refused, to slaughter him and his attendants, he at length consented to attempt an escape. To the Count and Countess de Spaur, the Duke d'Harcourt and the minister of Spain belongs the honour of having rescued the Head of the Church from the hands of his subjects. At dusk, on the 24th, D' Harcourt arrived at the Quirinal in his state carriage with postillions and torch bearers, and all the display that was certain to attract public attention. He demanded an audience with the Pope, and as ambassador of France was instantly admitted. Not a moment was to be lost. Instantly assuming the disguise that had been prepared for him, the venerable Pontiff, attended only by Fillipino, a faithful servant, passed the corridors and public staircases in safety, and quitted the palace by a small private door. A common hackney coach, provided by the duke for the occasion, was in waiting; His Holiness entered and was driven away without the least suspicion having been excited.

For two hours the ambassador, left alone in the audience chamber, kept up the innocent deceit of speaking aloud, as though engaged in a warm discussion. At the end of that time he came forth and, addressing the guards in the anti-room : "The Pope," he said, "is exceedingly weary ;

as you may imagine, he is greatly in need of repose ; do
not attempt to disturb him." Then, quitting the palace in
all haste, he drove to Civita Vecchia, embarked on board
the French war frigate, "Tenera," and steamed for Gaeta.

The Pontiff, in the meanwhile, had reached St. John
Lateran, where the Count de Spaur was impatiently
awaiting his arrival. They started together, and at midnight reached Albanum. There they were joined by the
countess and her almoner, and the whole party proceeded
with great rapidity towards the frontier. After passing
in safety a patrol of Carabineers, and narrowly escaping
detection at Fondi, they arrived at Terracina at five in
the morning. At daybreak they found themselves at
Gaeta, the first town of the kingdom of Naples.

During that long eventful night armed men surrounded
the Quirinal, the sentinels were at their posts in the
interior of the palace, the watchword had been given, the
officers duly went their rounds and reported that all was
secure. The vultures and ravens hooted and croaked
round the nest upon the rock, but the eagle had taken
flight.

Since the earliest times of the middle ages, the temporal
power of the Sovereign Pontiff has been the great object
of attack. The Counts of Tusculum attempted its overthrow, and when these passed away the whole force of the
German Emperors was directed towards the same object.
Succeeding these came Arnold of Brescia, and the great
tribune Rienzi, devoting intellectual power and physical
force to the work of stripping the Pope of that earthly
lordship which is the most legitimate to be found amongst
men. They all failed, and overthrew themselves in attempting the impossible task.

Will the cut-throats of Mazzini succeed? It cannot be, for the Pope out of Rome is the keystone taken from the edifice. It is the interest of Christendom that he should return to this essential position.

But why was Pius IX. driven into exile? Surely not for having reformed liberty, for he was its very leader in Italy. No, to the burning shame of the Roman people, this generous enlightened prince was violently dethroned for an act that was both moral courage and political wisdom, viz., refusal to go to war with Austria. He was the victim of that impious policy which boasts that among its arguments the one most convincing is "the dagger democratic and blessed."

But his people, for whom he had done and suffered so much, what is to be said of *them?*

Dr. Newman has written, "The minority in Rome is wicked, the majority are only cowardly and incapable." Another writer appears to have stated the truth more fully. Seven hundred years ago, St. Bernard wrote to Pope Eugenius the following letter :—

"What shall I say of your people? Why, that they are the Roman people. I could not more precisely or more fully say what I think of your subjects. What has been so notorious for ages as the wantonness of the Romans?—a race accustomed to tumult, a race cruel and unmanageable. . . . . Whom will you find of your city who received you as Pope without a bribe or the hopes of such? They promise to be trustworthy that they may be able to injure those who shall trust them. . . . . Odious to earth and Heaven, impious towards God, reckless towards things sacred, factious amongst themselves,

envious of their neighbours, inhuman towards foreigners,
. . . . restless till they gain an end, and ungrateful when
they have gained it. They have taught their tongues to
speak big words, while their performances are slight
indeed. . . . . Heartless tormentors of an old and
venerable man, to whom foreigners have shown themselves kinder than his own flesh and blood."

Has the character of these Romans improved with age ?

CHAPTER XIII.

On the morning of the 25th of November, 1848, Pius IX. entered the small Neapolitan town which was to afford him a safe retreat for many months. His first care was to communicate with the King of Naples, to whom he sent the following dignified letter :—

" Sir,—The enemies of the Holy See and of religion triumph at Rome. In order to avoid compromising his person and character, and lest his presence should appear to give a sanction to the excesses they are committing, the Chief of the Catholic Church has found himself compelled to abandon his capital. I do not know to what part of the globe the Divine Will, to which I submit, may conduct my steps ; in the meanwhile I have taken refuge in your Majesty's kingdom, attended by a few faithful adherents. I do not know what your sentiments may be in my regard ; I therefore think it right to inform you, through the Count de Spaur, the Bavarian Ambassador to the Holy See, that I am ready to quit the Neapolitan territory should my presence be a cause of political trouble to your Majesty."

The reply of Ferdinand was both princely and Catholic.

The masters of the palace received orders to prepare
instantly from the royal wardrobe everything that it
seemed probable the illustrious exile might need. The
gold and silver plate of the King's table were sent down
to the port for embarkation; the steam frigates, the
"Robert" and the "Tancred," with one regiment of
Grenadiers and a battalion of the line, were ready for sea
in a few hours.

"We will be the bearer of our own answer, Count,"
said the good monarch. And in truth, to the amazement
of the inhabitants of Gaeta (who were ignorant of the
presence of the Pope in their town), towards noon of the
26th, King Ferdinand, accompanied by his Queen, Count
Aquila, the Infant Don Sebastian, and a numerous suite,
landed at Gaeta, and proceeded to the obscure hotel in
which the Pontiff had concealed himself since his arrival.
And there, kneeling at the feet of Pius, the King gave
thanks to Heaven that he had been chosen to shelter and
defend its own anointed servant.

When Napoleon the Great was in the midst of his
wonderful successes, and forgot that all power comes from
God alone, he wrote to the Pope of the time, saying, "All
Italy must belong to me." When he uttered these words,
nearly the whole of Europe was indeed his. And, seized
with the spirit of Haman, with the world at his feet, he
yet could not endure that there should be found one single
man not acknowledging his right to possess everything.
So he wrote: "Rome must be mine, as well as all the
rest."

What was the answer he received from the Head of the
Catholic Church? "You mistake; there is to be no
Emperor in Rome." It was the protest of right against

brute force. And when by violence Napoleon had succeeded in placing the tricolor on St. Angelo, and had
issued that famous decree which declared the Roman
States to be part of universal France, there came another
sort of answer from the same dauntless voice—the public
excommunication of the Emperor of the world. In this
noble document we find words very applicable to the
present state of Italian policy : " The temporal power is
not ours to dispose of; we only administer it."

These events occurred in the years 1805-1809. Only
six years later, upon the rock of St. Helena, without
power, and a captive for life, was to be seen the former
conqueror of Italy and Spain, of Germany and Egypt.
And his story could be told in one sentence. In the
intoxication of his ambition it had moved that which, in
falling, had power to crush him.

Why do we go so far back ? Only to make the assertion
more for..bly evident, that men, when their passions are
roused, nearly always forget the lessons of history.

The news of the flight of Pius IX. from his capital was
the signal throughout Protestant countries for the
greatest rejoicing. The one cry was, " The Papacy has
come to an end."

" Why to an end ? " asked many a sad-hearted but
loyal Catholic.

And the answer invariably was, " Because the Pope has
fled; he has lost his throne; his people have cast him
off."

" But did such a catastrophe never happen in Christendom before ? And, if so, did it put an end to the Papacy,
or did it so much as diminish the temporal power ? "

" Alas ! no ; we cannot say that it did."

Admirable and daring logicians, then, who prove an assertion by a fact that has nothing in the world to do with it !

In the case of Pius IX. we know exactly what happened, in spite of the expectations of his enemies. His flight to Naples gave occasion for the exhibition to the whole world of how mighty is the power wielded by the successor of St. Peter. In every tongue spoken under heaven there came to him words of sympathy, and loving offers of assistance. The letter addressed to him by the French Republic proved that France is always heart and soul Catholic France. Louis Napoleon, then candidate for the Presidentship, wrote thus to the Nuncio :—

"The temporal sovereignty of the venerable Chief of the Church is bound up with Catholicity as with the safety of Italy."

Every Catholic people sent a deputation to express at once their fidelity to him and their detestation for the treason of his own people. From one end of Christendom to the other there was heard the loud expression of grief for the sufferings of Pius, mingled with significant denunciations. And soon the flags of all nations were seen waving in the port of Gaeta, and the representatives from the Old and New Worlds transformed this little fortress town into one of the most brilliant Courts of Europe.

"It is a matter of history," said the *Times* of December, '49, "that at the very hour of his fall Pius IX. is more entirely and essentially Pope and Head of the Church than many hundreds of his predecessors amidst all the splendour of the Lateran."

Gaeta for the time was Rome, for Rome itself had become a den of thieves. Two days after his arrival at

Gaeta, the Pontiff issued a proclamation, addressed to his rebellious subjects :—

"The violence offered us in these latter days has compelled us to separate ourselves from our people for a time. Amongst the motives that have determined us to this, was the most powerful one, that we might be left with the fullest liberty in the exercise of the supreme authority of the Holy See, which the Catholic world, under present circumstances, might well suppose not to be free in our hands. . . . We cannot, without treason to our duties, abstain from protesting solemnly that we have been defeated by violence. And therefore we declare all acts null and void and of no legal force performed by those who have seized our power. . . . . Yet, having at heart not to leave Rome without a chief or a Government in our absence, we nominate a Commission of the following : Cardinal Castracane, Monsignore Roberti, Prince Barbarini, the Marquis de Bologna, Ricci de Macerata, and Lieutenant-General Zacchi.

"Pius P.P. IX.

"Given at Gaeta, 27th November, 1848."

This proclamation was not known in Rome till the 7th of December. The revolutionists had used every effort to conceal it, for it was the destruction of the falsehood which they had already circulated through the States, to the effect that they had been appointed the guardians of Rome by the Pontiff himself. So far from having in any way sanctioned the temporary rule of those who had compelled him to flight, Pius did not allow the Revolution one hour of prescriptive right. Every public act of

government on the part of the latter was instantly
annulled by a proclamation from Gaeta, while, at the
same time, Europe proclaimed by her policy what, in a
few months, she was going to maintain by force of arms,
viz., that the Pope out of Rome is not therefore dethroned.
It was at Gaeta during the exile, not at Rome, that the
Ambassadors and representatives of all the Powers met
and consulted.

For the Sovereign Pontiff was there; and Religion, to
whom he belongs, and whose capital is the Eternal City,
recognized no right in a band of infidel assassins either
to take the crown from the head of the Successor of St.
Peter, or to govern in that place where it forbids them so
much as to live.

It is also a fact of modern history, that whatever it
chose to call itself, " Provisional Government," " Roman
Constitution," or the " Republic," the usurped authority
of the Mazzinians in Rome during the few disastrous
months of its existence, received no note of recognition,
no word of sympathy, no sign of respect from any Government, from any Christian people. Rome, for the time,
was as a city struck with the plague, a leprous place,
cut off from all society with the healthy and the living.
The rule of Mazzini was a usurpation of violence, which
was allowed to endure only whilst Europe sharpened her
weapons. It vanished before the chivalry of Christendom, as the vapours of corruption before the face of the
sun; and those leaders (the modern Scipios and Gracchi) of
the deluded wretches, whom they left to ruin and death,
sunk like lead into their first obscurity, and all the deeper
on account of their short unnatural elevation.

" O Rome, Rome! God is my witness, that each

by this faction of demagogues. After enumerating the benefits he had bestowed on his ungrateful subjects, the Pope said:—" We declare null and void every act of this usurpation ; this Junta has no authority."

But in a few days appeared a more solemn document, viz., the excommunication of the 1st of January, uttered against the Government and its abettors, and with which all who should take part in voting for any member of that illegal assembly were also threatened. The revolutionists were in a panic.

It seemed as though some resistless power was dogging their footsteps, and reading their very thoughts, ready to thwart by anticipation every foul design. They were well aware that Pius IX. was not forgotten though banished, and they also knew that the bulk of the people had sufficient faith left to believe in the power both to paralyze and destroy that accompanies the anathema of the chief priest of Christendom.

Wherever the Government edicts were affixed, there also, in a few hours, were to be seen copies of the protests and the excommunication. It was in vain to tear them down, or to threaten with death all who should make them public ; they were found every day replaced, no one knew, or rather no one cared to tell.* And as the people read them, a sense of the evil to which at least they had consented, filled their minds, accompanied by a terror of punishment near at hand. The wife of Armellini rushed into her husband's presence in the midst of a

* It was Vincent Lumaca, a devoted adherent of Pius IX., who contrived, with the assistance of a few faithful companions, to print and publish throughout Rome every proclamation issued by his exiled Prince. During the usurpation Lumaca, at great risk, went frequently to Gaeta under a variety of disguises.

banquet, holding in her hand the excommunication of
Jan. 1. "Unhappy wretch," she exclaimed, "do you
sit there feasting when Heaven is cursing you? See,.
Pius IX. has called down God against you!" In a word,
the Roman Republic, as a Government, was without all
power from the moment that the voice of the Pontiff was
raised against it from his place of exile. The strength of
right neutralized the violence of wrong.

In the meanwhile, the day for the Roman elections
had been fixed upon as an opportunity for impressing the
people by a grand demonstration.

In the square of the Capitol, which was brilliantly
illuminated, was held this patriotic feast in honour of
"pure democracy." The traitors of the Civic Guard
were on duty keeping the ground, and by sound of
trumpet and the discharge of cannon the names of the
chosen ones of the happy Roman States were to be proclaimed in the face of the world. Never has been
witnessed in modern times so solemn a farce and so
ridiculous a failure.

To the amazement of the Executive Committee the
majority of the population abstained from voting altogether. Only 20,000 votes were recorded for the whole
of Rome, and of these it is said, "Many were the same
persons hired to vote in different wards."

In Citta di Castello and Corneto, not a single vote was
recorded.

At Sinigaglia (the Pope's birthplace) 200 persons only
voted out of a population of 27,500, and most of these
recorded their names for the Sovereign Pontiff. The
same took place throughout the "Legations."

An act such as this was not to be mistaken; it was the

others into danger, and staying himself in safety and arranging plots for them. Some of the edicts issued by the three villains into whose clutches the miserable Romans had fallen could hardly be surpassed for folly, and brought upon their authors the contempt and laughter of Europe. We venture to give one or two samples :—

"12th April, 1849.—The Triumvirs decree : 'The Po is the national river.'

(Signed) "MAZZINI.
"ARMELLINI.
"SAFFI."

"13th April, 1849.—The Triumvirs decree : ' Considering late events, the Roman Republic shall never pass away.' (Signed) "&c."

"14th April, 1849.—'The Triumvirs swear in the name of God and the people that the country shall be saved.' (Signed) "MAZZINI, &c."

By the side of this ridiculous document appeared next morning the following reply :—

"15th April, 1849.—'We swear that the three scoundrels who oppress Rome are publicly perjured ; for on account of their crimes and follies the country is already ruined.' (Signed) "PASQUIN."*

* Pasquino was a cobbler who lived in Rome more than three hundred years ago, and was celebrated for his witty repartees. After his death a statue was dug up near his house, and placed in the entrance of the palace of the Ursini. The populace called this statue Pasquino, and satirical notices were affixed to it, making them in this way the sayings of Pasquino : hence our word " Pasquinade."

However, he who forgetting the doctrines of "liberty and equality" did not show himself averse to the absurd title of "King of Rome," given him by the mad mob, had already proved that if he could not save, he thoroughly understood how to spoliate and rob. As we have seen above, during Mazzini's brief authority the churches were pillaged of their gold and silver treasures, and the very sepulchres were rifled in search of supposed hidden wealth. Money worthy of the name disappeared altogether, and was replaced by "Mazzinian notes," from 100 dollars to 1 dollar, and from 40 cents to 10 cents.

The "Mistress of the Nations" had become a wilderness. Trade, there was none; credit, of course, was at an end; the dwellings on all sides were deserted; the streets were filled with hordes of starving miscreants, who now at length must thoroughly have understood the grandeur of Rome when "regenerated by revolution."

And, as if to crown all this misery and crime with a last horrible blasphemy, on Easter Sunday, 1849, in the balcony of S. Peter's, occupying the place of the Sovereign Pontiff, and bearing the Blessed Sacrament in his unholy hands, appeared the apostate monk Gavazzi; and he blessed the drunken mob that was reeling to and fro beneath, shouting the "Marseillaise" and the "Ça Ira."

The end was drawing near; Catholic Europe, with her eyes averted in horror of these atrocities, was already springing forward, her hand upon her sword.

CHAPTER XV.

When Louis Philippe was driven from the throne of
France and compelled to take refuge in England, Europe
looked on with the most complete indifference. When
the Emperor of Austria fled from his capital into the
Tyrol, the world regarded the event with provoking
complacency. When, too, the Italian and German
Princes lost their principalities, no nation seemed to
care or wonder. But the conduct of Europe, both
people and statesmen, was very different in the case
of the Sovereign Pontiff and the flight to Gaeta. The
reason for this has been already given by the deepest
thinker of the age:—" Rome is the religious centre of
millions, who care little for the Romans themselves,
but immensely for the treasures of which they are the
guardians." Spain was the first to manifest in public
this solicitude.

Soon after the appeal issued in the early part of 1849,
in the name of the Pontiff, calling on the Catholic
Powers to come to the rescue of the patrimony of the
Church, the Court of Spain addressed the different
Governments of Europe on the same subject.

"The Catholic Powers," it said, "have always considered themselves pledged to maintain the temporal sovereignty of the Pope, a subject of such importance to Europe that it cannot be left a prey to so small a portion of the Catholic world as the Roman States."

The question thus started soon became the all-absorbing one in every Cabinet. In the French Chambers especially, the dispute upon it rose high, for there the Republican faction was still powerful, and did its utmost through the eloquence of its advocates, Jules Favre and Victor Hugo, to induce the French Government to abstain from all intervention between the Pope and the revolutionists. It was in vain. France, whatever may be said to the contrary, is at heart Catholic, and the nation, as one man, responded to the eloquent call of Montalembert and others that they should go to the succour of "the most ancient, most legitimate, and holiest of sovereignties."

After a few precious weeks wasted in matters of form the plenipotentiaries appointed to arrange the terms of the intervention met at Gaeta, at which place Pius had signified his wish that the Congress should be held. On the 30th March, 1849, the representatives of France, Austria, Spain, and Naples, opened the Conference, whose decisions were to be of such moment to Catholic interests.

To the invitation which was sent him as a monarch ruling over a Catholic people, the King of Sardinia sent an evasive reply, through Gioberti, to the effect that Sardinia could not be a party to any Conference to which Austria was admitted. This, at the commencement of his reign, was ominous of the future; yet, after all, it was more consistent that he, who was afterwards to be the despoiler of the Church, should have no share in the glory of the restoration of the Pontiff to the throne of St. Peter.

The deliberations at Gaeta were of short duration. The question to be considered was the simplest possible. It was to be either an armed intervention to restore the Pope, or nothing. No one so much as hinted at granting a hearing to the revolutionists; on the contrary, it was felt that to attempt to treat with Mazzini would have been to insult human nature.

In a few days, the result of the Conference was made known to Europe. The Catholic Powers had resolved that Pius IX. should be restored; that the chief honour of the enterprize should be entrusted to the arms of France; and that Austria, Spain, and Naples should be ready with effective aid, to meet any extraordinary contingency.

The army of Cavaignac had long been massed at the foot of the Alps. It was now to march to the most glorious of its battle-fields. The enemies of the Pontiff and of Catholicity clung, indeed, to one last hope. It seemed to them very questionable whether the soldiers of that Republic which had expelled Louis Philippe would be willing to fight against those who had driven into exile the Pope-King. It was strange they could not comprehend the wide difference that existed between the two cases. Frenchmen, whatever they may think about Paris ruling France, hold, as a rule, that Rome belongs to the Christian world, France included. They who calculated on the defection of the French troops in this instance, forgot that the men who were about to start on the Roman expedition had, a few months before, seen their comrades shot down, and such as were taken prisoners shamefully

mutilated, by these very men whom they were now marching to destroy. A fiercer enemy to the Red Republican
could scarcely be conceived than the French infantry
soldier of 1849, with the scene of the slaughter in the
streets of Paris fresh in his recollection.

Notwithstanding this certain fact, during the whole
siege of Rome the conspirators outside the city (English
as well as French) were frequently discovered endeavouring to tamper with the fidelity of the besieging army.
Instead of the court-martial and hanging, which these so
richly merited, they were, as a rule, contemptuously dismissed by Oudinot and his officers, to carry to their
patron, Lord Palmerston, the account of their failure and
escape.

On the 24th April, part of the French expedition, under
the command of General Oudinot, came in sight of Civita
Vecchia. On the the next day, the disembarkation commenced.* To their great surprise, no opposition was made
by the inhabitants; on the contrary, they were received
with cries of "Long live the French and Pius IX.!"
Oudinot had been given to understand that he must prepare for a stout resistance at Civita Vecchia, but that he
would meet with none at Rome. Just the reverse took
place. The Duke d'Harcourt had written to him from
Gaeta: "In spite of the Roman rhodomontade, you will
have no enemy to encounter." All gave him the same
assurance, and this fatal mistake was the cause of much
after bloodshed.

On taking possession of Civita Vecchia, the French
commander issued a proclamation, at once peaceable and

* Ten thousand rifles, sent from England to arm the Roman populace, were captured by the French a few hours after landing.

into Rome a few days before the arrival of the first de-
tachment of the French army, terrified the wretched
inhabitants into the resolution of offering a savage resistance.   He brought with him an army of strangers,
collected from Piedmont, Hungary, Poland, and England,
the scum of Europe, the desperadoes of the Revolution,
who cared nothing for Rome or the Romans, but who
regarded a protracted struggle on this battlefield of
socialism as their only escape from utter destruction.
Neither did their hopes of success appear altogether
visionary.   The fortifications of the city were strong,
and defended by more than one hundred pieces of cannon.
The troops they could depend upon numbered at least
17,000, and were most of them men well practised in
street fighting, and skilful in availing themselves of all
the chances which occur so frequently in barricade warfare.   Added to this was the well-founded hope that their
allies in the French Chambers, though foiled once, might
at last succeed in obtaining the recall of the expedition,
or at least might so obstruct its efforts by the interference
of diplomacy as to disgust and dishearten both army and
commander.

With all these expectations bright upon them, Garibaldi
and his fierce associates in arms hurled defiance at the
soldiers of " the eldest daughter of the Church."

CHAPTER XVI.

On the 30th of April, the army of France took up its
position under the walls of Rome, on the plateau which
commands the Pertuzza gate of the city, though the siege-
train and many of the regiments of the line, on their way
to join their comrades, were still far from the scene of
action.

It had been the intention of the French commander to
make a last solemn appeal for peace to the Triumvirs.
To this he was urged by a twofold motive. He knew it
to be particularly the desire of his Government that, if
possible, he should act as mediator, to prevent war; he
was also well aware of the odium which would attach to
his memory if, through any fault on his part, the monuments of antiquity and of Christian art in which Rome
abounds should be destroyed. It was this delicate sense
of the sacredness that attaches to the treasures contained
in the capital of the Catholic world which for a while
restrained the French commander from proceeding to
extremities against Rome, and was the cause of the attack

upon the city being made on that side where, by nature and art, it is nearly impregnable.

Writing to the Minister of War at Paris some days after the siege had regularly commenced, Oudinot says : "The howitzers have not as yet been used, out of respect for the Roman monuments ; yet the Republicans state, contrary to truth, that our projectiles have destroyed the *chefs d'œuvre* of Raphael." General le Vaillant, also writing to the same official, said : "Attacking the city by the road that leads from the gate of St. Pancras is full of danger, but then we run the less risk of damaging the public monuments—a very powerful reason when attacking with cannon a city like Rome, which includes the history of the civilized world."

This Christian chivalry was the cause of great loss of life to the French army. Let the reader contrast with it the conduct of the revolutionists, themselves mostly Italian. At the Villa Albani, Garibaldi ordered the wonderful collection of the masterpieces of Grecian and Roman art, the property of Cardinal Allessandro, to be given to the flames. In addition to this, during the siege, by orders of the same Vandal, the Villas Borghesi, Patrizzi, and Torlonia were sacked ; all the buildings to the right of the Theatre of Apollo, greater part of those near St. Angelo, and the Hospital de Spirito Santo were razed to the ground ; and the frescos of Raphael were destroyed.

But to resume. The head of the French advancing column no sooner came within reach of the fire of the besieged, than it was vehemently attacked by the latter with a fury as sudden as it was unexpected.

Ill supported, and with no artillery, the soldiers of "*la grande nation*" maintained for hours their traditional

The French Army
Oudinot—Contr.
regards the M...
French—Joy i...
ordered to tak...
Sortie by Gar...
The Midnigh...
Council of W...
—Last Assa...

On the :...
position u...
commands
train and ...
to join th...
action.

It had
make a ...
To this ...
to be p...
possible,
was als...

night the whole city of Rome was illumined
. r of the Triumvirate, and the giddy populace,
 .ited with this unlooked-for success, gave way
delirious joy, and believed their leaders when
told them that the besieging army was in full
t, and that a few days more and then they, the
ndants of the conquerors of the world, would rush
ı from their fortifications and sweep the last of the
d invaders from the sacred Italian soil.
'asquino, however, was not nearly so sanguine. The
rning after the rejoicings the following biting jest
peared on his column : " Rejoice, O happy people,
cause they who have taken from you your last bajoccho,
.ve you liberty, either to have your throats cut by the
rench, or, if you like not that, you may negotiate for
your death with their own chosen Zambianchi, who kills
priests for recreation."

After the repulse at the gate of St. Pancras, the French
troops spent two days in organizing their camp.

Oudinot fixed his headquarters at Paolo, a small
village of twenty houses. There he established his
military hospital, and having cantoned his forces in
perfect safety, patiently awaited the arrival of the
artillery and the remaining regiments of the expedition. These reached the camp on the 4th of May, and
raised the besieging army to the number of 25,000 men.
Being now fully prepared to enter upon the desperate
task before him, the French general had resolved without
delay to push on vigorously the siege works, when he
nd himself suddenly arrested by an unexpected
onent. M. de Lesseps, the envoy of the French
vernment, had arrived at Rome, armed with the

most imprudent instructions, and amongst others, with
the order to treat, if possible, with the Triumvirate.
Without a word to Oudinot, he concluded an armistice
with the besieged, during which, he said, he hoped to
settle the whole "Italian question" by peaceful discussion.

The result of this folly was in the end most disastrous.
It gave time to the besieged to complete their prepara-
tions.   While it lasted, the defenders of Rome were
recruited by numerous bands from Lombardy ; assurances
came from the revolutionists in every place that France
was really on their side, that the warlike demonstration
was merely for political purposes, and that the besieged
had but to stand firmly for a few weeks, and in all probability the Republic would be recognized by Europe.
Had De Lesseps been in the pay of the revolutionists he
could not have served them better.

Against any such charge as this his admirers have ever
vehemently protested, yet it must be admitted his silli-
ness had all the appearance of treason.   France had not
been called into Italy with a large army in order to
protect, but simply to destroy—to destroy that which
denies law, liberty, property and religion, and which, if
it be not swept from the earth, will render civilized
existence impossible.

The armistice of M. de Lesseps lasted until the French
army was decimated by fever, and the survivors dis-
heartened for the terrible work that was soon to be
required of them.   Yet, with their usual mendacity,
the Romans, in their reports of the siege, declared that
the result might have been different "had they not been
taken by surprise when totally unprepared."

In the meanwhile, Oudinot, disgusted with the false
position in which he found himself placed, yet bound by
the suspension of arms agreed to by the envoy, wrote to
his Government a soldier-like statement of the difficult
situation of affairs, in which, after enumerating his own
grievances, he declared that, the arms of France having
suffered a repulse, it was a point of honour that such
should be atoned for; but that diplomacy was standing
in the way, to the bitter regret alike of men and officers.
The answer he received was at once consoling to his
feelings as a man and a soldier. He was ordered to take
Rome forthwith, at any cost, and to consider himself in
reality, what he already was in name, the responsible
head of the whole expedition.

The Triumvirs, understanding what instructions had
come from Paris, and foreseeing the certain fate which
awaited them from war, now laboured hard to make
terms ; but in spite of the disloyal assistance which they
received from De Lesseps, who endeavoured to persuade
the general to a convention, their attempts completely
failed. The reply of Oudinot was sternly unalterable :

"On the 1st of June the siege will formally begin;
until then I will respect the armistice of M. de Lesseps,
in which I had no part; but my only terms are, surrender
at discretion."

It had been evident from the first to the French com-
manders, that the execution of siege works against Rome
would be perfectly vain, so long as the enemy was left in
possession of the heights of St. Pancras, and also the
entrenched positions which they held round the villas
Corsini and Valentini. It was resolved, therefore, to
attempt to dislodge him from this favourable post, as a

preliminary to slower and more scientific operations. At
three o'clock in the morning of June 3rd, Le Vaillant,
with a body of picked troops, advanced to assail these
formidable works. He was met with a resistance worthy
of his attack, for the besieged, who knew the value of the
position which they were defending, fought with a desperation which, for a time, seemed to promise success. But
the *furia Franchese* was upon them; not a man of the
assailants but had vowed never to return except as victor
from that awful encounter, and as the murderous fire
from the forts, the entrenchments, and the walls, mowed
down their ranks, the survivors formed in closer column,
pressing forward to the cry of " Vive la France !" " Vive
le Pape Roy !" Before such enthusiasm everything went
down, and after two hours of the bloodiest struggle that
this campaign witnessed, the shattered remnant of the
assaulting party found itself master of the whole line of
defence. Again and again, during the siege, and often in
the darkness of the night, did the revolutionists attempt
to recover this vantage ground which they had lost; but
the tricolor flag, that waved upon the heights, never for
one instant was moved from its haughty place.

From the 4th to the 11th of June, nothing occurred
above frequent skirmishes between the sharpshooters on
both sides; but on the latter day a furious sortie was
made upon the besiegers. No less than 6000 men, headed
by Garibaldi in person, and protected by an unceasing
cannonade, passed suddenly from the gates of the city in
the hopes of overwhelming the attacking forces by the
vehemence and unexpectedness of their onslaught. They
were gallantly met by Colonel Neil, who, with two columns
of infantry, forced them back into the city, after they had

my hotel, and all other French establishments.   Confide in my vigilance."

The pestilent spirit of vanity was paramount in this man.   The Republicans cared no more for the French flag than for that of St. Peter.   Even M. de Lesseps himself was soon made to feel in what very small consideration he was held by them when no longer able to be their tool.   He was publicly threatened with assassination for having failed in obtaining for them advantageous terms— a hard fate, when we consider that he had sacrificed his character as a loyal Frenchman in the service of their cause.   To add to his disappointments, he was soon after recalled by his own Government, M. de Courcelles, a very different man, being appointed in his stead.   The latter at once gave the Republican leaders to understand that he was thoroughly in accord with Oudinot, and that all hope of treating with him was therefore fallacious.

Matters had thus at last reached the climax.   On the 29th of June, the Feast of SS. Peter and Paul, the French had penetrated into the quarter of the Janiculum.   The enemy, indeed, still held some bastions, which they seemed resolved to defend foot by foot; but on the morning of the 30th, Espinasse, famous in African warfare, led his men, before daybreak, against these formidable works, and carried them all at the point of the bayonet.   Masters of these and of the Gate of St. Pancras, the French were, in fact, masters of Rome; and therefore, after a last vain attempt to obtain terms, the besieged submitted to surrender at discretion.

Garibaldi, with 3000 men, escaped by the Gate of St. John to Albanum, loaded with booty stolen from the churches and convents.   Thence he made his way to Lodi,

where his brigands committed every excess.   Mazzini had
already fled to Switzerland.   The Constituent Assembly
resigned into the hands of the French commander that
power which it had never for one moment lawfully held.

The reign of terror had ceased, and on the 3rd of July,
1849, at the Palace Portici, Colonel Neil presented himself before the Supreme Pontiff, and in the name of
Catholic France laid at his feet the keys of the liberated
City of St. Peter.

CHAPTER XVII.

The Siege of Rome lasted twenty-six days. By good
fortune partly, and also in a great measure from the
method of advance and attack expressly adopted for
such a purpose by the French commander, nearly all
the monuments of the Eternal City had escaped injury,
at least from the besiegers. The only works of antiquity
as well as of modern art that suffered were those which
were designedly destroyed, as we have elsewhere stated,
by the revolutionists themselves. To quote the words of
the M. de Courcelles's dispatch to the French Minister of
War :—

" No ancient monument nor museum has been injured
by us. Some buildings, etc., have been destroyed by the
insurgents."

The official report, drawn up by Colonel Neil for the
National Assembly, contains the same assertion, and
contradicts directly Lord Palmerston's agent, Freeborn,
who had stated that " the ravages in Rome had been
caused by the French army."

" Freeborn," says Montalembert, " has opposed to
these criminating documents a prudent silence."

On the 3rd of July General Oudinot entered the

conquered city, at the head of his staff and amid the
acclamations of the people. The cry of "Pius IX. for
ever!" was strangely mingled by that fickle populace
with shouts of "Long live the French!" It may, indeed,
have been that feeling their deliverance from the revolutionary oppression and from all the horrors which had
lately surrounded them, the voice of the Roman mob
came, for once, from the heart. Still, we cannot forget
the sentence agreed on by those best acquainted with
these degenerate descendants of the masters of the world,
"The modern Roman has no political mind, but he is
good at shouting." However, if with them external
manifestation at all expresses truly internal emotion, the
French troops had good reason to be satisfied with their
first reception.

Six hours after the entry of the conquerors not a
barricade was left standing. The people, who were in a
starving condition, were glad to be employed in any
work that would cause money to re-appear; and as the
French general paid scrupulously for everything, labour
included, the Romans themselves in a few days had removed from every street all signs of the past siege.

The 15th of July was fixed upon by Oudinot for the
formal proclamation of the restored power of the Sovereign
Pontiff. To the discharge of a hundred pieces of cannon,
and amidst the vivas of the whole population, the Papal
flag was officially planted on the Capitol, while at St.
eter's (the world's Cathedral), *Te Deum* was chanted in
thanksgiving for the return of order and religion. On
this day, a workman (Annibali Piccioli), in the presence
of the assembled thousands, read an address of thanks, in
the name of the Roman people, to the soldiers and officers

of the army of France, for having delivered their city from the tyranny of the Triumvirs, and the ferocity of the brigands of Garibaldi.

In the meanwhile, the cause of justice was equally successful throughout the States. As early as May, the Austrians had proclaimed the Pontifical Government at Ferrara, Forli, Bologna and Ravenna. Sabelli had already effected the restoration in Urbino and Peraro. The frigates of Spain also had appeared off Terracina, threatening to bombard the town unless the red flag of the Republicans was removed and the Papal colours hoisted in its place. On all sides the Catholic power was making itself felt, and was exacting reparation for the outrage of the Pontiff's exile.

A few days after the surrender of Rome, a proclamation came from Gaeta, in which Pius IX. named a commission with full powers to act in his absence, in the regulation of all civil affairs. This commission consisted of Cardinals Sartuci, Casani, and Altieri, who entered upon their duties on the 31st of July. Their first act was necessarily to annul all the proceedings of the late usurpation; their next was to recall the worthless paper money, which Mazzini had compelled the people to accept in exchange for their gold and silver and other valuables. But the kindly spirit of the master shone through the deeds of the subordinates. Sartucci declared what would be the character of the acts of himself and fellow-commissioners when he 'said : "Knowing the heart of Pius IX. we have decided, as much as possible, not to look backwards, but to endeavour to throw a veil over the past."

So strictly was this clement policy carried out, that in

the French Chambers Tocqueville was able to silence the
Republicans during the debate of October, '49, with this
sentence: "The 'Roman Republic' began in assassination, but the Pontifical Restoration has been accomplished
without a single person, for political reasons, losing property, liberty, or life."

On the 3rd of August, Oudinot surrendered the entire
civil administration of the city into the hands of the
appointed Commission, at the same time naming General
Rostolan military governor of Rome. In their address to
the inhabitants of the Pontifical States, the Cardinal Com-
missioners affirmed that which had been already declared
by Neil and De Courcelles in their official reports, viz.,
that "the ancient and modern works of art, and all those
things that belong to the civilized world, have been spared
by the French."

We think that sufficient has now been adduced to show
that for whatever was destroyed in Rome the besieging
army cannot be held accountable; and when it is also
remembered that at the end of the siege Garibaldi absolutely proposed that the city and all it contained should
be demolished, we imagine that the fair-minded reader
will not have much difficulty in determining who were
the guilty parties in any act of vandalism that took place.

While society in Rome was reassuming the aspect of
civilization, and men were beginning to feel once more
that their property and lives were their own, the defeated
revolutionists were plotting in their hiding-places how
to foment suspicion and hatred between the conquerors
and the vanquished. Garibaldi, indeed, was no longer
with them. Driven from the environs of Rome by General
Morris, and with the Spaniards and Austrians upon his

trail, he had gained, with the remnant of his band, the
mountains that traverse the Abruzzi.

The less daring conspirator, Mazzini, had also, as we
have seen, effected his escape in safety. The head and
the hand were for a time lost to the Red Republicans of
Rome. Still, there were left disciples enough of the same
school, who were ready to seize any opportunity for
endeavouring to excite to tumult and bloodshed. At first
they contented themselves with satire; to this succeeded
denunciation. The walls of the city were everywhere
placarded with the coarsest lampoons upon the French
soldier, accompanied with warnings to the Roman people
not to trust to professions of friendship, which, they said,
were only used as a disguise to lull suspicion until the
moment for their destruction should be ready. By means
such as these the revolutionists hoped to excite bad blood
between the foreign soldier and the citizen. A popular
tumult, an affray with the military could hardly take
place without much loss of life, and this would suffice to
furnish the Republican cause with a sort of argument,
and to excite debate in the different Cabinets of Europe,
particularly in that of France, where the chief strength
of the revolutionary party was known to lie.

We present our readers with one out of the many
insulting placards posted about Rome, for the purpose of
irritating the invading army :—

"For the days of Order.

"Soldiers of the Mediterranean and of the Holy
Water: You left France as Republicans, you will re-
enter it as Cossacks of the sacristy, which is 'the anti-
chamber to Paradise.' Each of you will carry home a

Capuchin friar in his haversack. God is great, and
Guizot, Thiers, Falloux, and Montalembert are His pro-
phets. Soldiers, by order of your allies, the Czar of
Russia and the Emperor of Austria, you are here. Cain
ought to kill Abel. The lion being overthrown, the ass
may safely kick him. Soldiers, be proud of having
helped at this courageous work."

It is to the honour of the brave men of the Roman expedition, that, with all the power in their hands, they did
not allow themselves any retaliation for these dastardly
insults. And their self-restraint had its reward. In the
eyes of the Roman bourgeois, the perfect discipline of the
French soldiers was a glad spectacle after the licence of
the Garibaldian hordes. He now beheld no act of
pillage, no rioting, and for whatever he was asked to
sell, ready money was offered. The shrewd shopkeeper
of the Corso was not long in discovering the superiority of
an honest Frenchman over a dishonest Italian.

Mazzini, indeed, had written from his safe retreat,
calling upon the Romans to imitate the noble conduct
of the Lombards who, in 1848, had refused to smoke the
Austrian cigars lest they should be benefiting the ex-
chequer of the enemy. So the "hero of the *café*" wrote
to Rome, saying, "Have nothing to do either with
French money or French produce."

This magnanimous advice, coming from one who had
enriched himself by the spoliation of their city, was too
much for the Roman gravity, and was consequently held
up to ridicule from one end of the patrimony to the
other. The statue of Pasquino answered Mazzini with
this mocking satire :—

CHAPTER XIX.

Whilst the Sovereign Pontiff was directing his energies to repair the desolation brought upon the States by the Revolution, new causes of anxiety were springing up on every side. In Belgium, the Ministry of Rogier and Frère was already attacking the Church, by impeding charitable legacies, by endeavouring to secularize education, and by opposing the clergy. At Turin also the same fatal power was at work. Indeed, throughout the whole of Piedmont, the anti-Catholic, we should say anti-Christian, movement was in rapid progress, encouraged without disguise by the Minister Brofferio, chief of the Radicals. In the capital of this once religious State, the priests were hissed in the pulpits, and were held up to ridicule upon the stage; parodies of the "Stabat Mater" and of the "Via Crucis" were sung in the streets; while every bookstall was heaped with works that had professedly for their object the scoffing at all religion, and the corrupting the morals of the young.

The Archbishop of Turin having refused the last sacraments to the Minister Santa Rossa, who had despoiled the Church, was first imprisoned and then exiled, and the episcopal property confiscated. The Servite fathers

also, who had obeyed the Archbishop's commands in the
case of this public offender and impenitent sinner Rossa,
were expelled from their monastery.

In all this Piedmont violated her own constitution of
1848, as may be seen from a perusal of Articles 24, 26, 27,
29, 400, 403 and 564, and also Article 4 of the Penal Code.

In his allocution of May 20th, 1850, in which he
publicly thanked the four powers that had come to his
assistance, Pius IX. denounced the acts of the infidel
ministry of Turin, declared them null and void, and
warned both Piedmont and Belgium of the ruin they
were surely preparing for themselves, by severing their
populations from the Church.   His words fell upon deaf
ears.   For twenty years have the Governments of these
two Catholic countries persevered in a policy which,
attacking the foundations of society, must have already
undermined the throne.

In the midst of these matters, of most serious import,
there sprung up a slight difficulty between the Pontifical
Government and Lord Palmerston, which involved the
latter in infinite ridicule.

The English who were in Rome during the days of the
siege had fraternized openly with the revolutionists, had
in every way displayed approbation of their violent acts.
But notwithstanding this patent fact, no sooner were order
and peace restored, than indemnity was demanded of the
Pope for the injuries which the English residents had
sustained.   The boon companion of the drayman Cicerovacchio, Lord Minto, who said he had returned to Rome by
invitation from the Pontiff himself,* and Freeborn, the

* "We are authorized to declare that the Holy Father has never
invited Lord Minto to Italy."—*Giornali di Roma.*

Catholic Relief Bill (1846) Lord Russell said : "I believe
we may repeal all that prevents a Roman Catholic Archbishop assuming a title held by a Bishop of the Established
Church; as to preventing persons assuming particular titles,
nothing could be more absurd and purile." Yet the very
same man on February 7th, 1851, brought in a Bill to the
House of Commons to prevent (under penalties) the
assumption of certain ecclesiastical titles.

The storm has since passed away, and having thoroughly
disgraced themselves in the eyes of the civilized world,
our countrymen have subsided into their usual state of
complete indifference with regard to religion altogether.
But English Catholics will never cease to remember with
gratitude and to pronounce with reverence the name of
the illustrious Pontiff who created them into "a body
politic out of a mere collection of individuals, taking them
from their unformed state and making them a Church."

It is no longer Canterbury and York and Exeter and
Salisbury; it is Westminster and Southwark and Beverley
and Salford; for the true Church has always the power
of placing her own landmarks.

CHAPTER XX.

Since the year 1815 the Catholics of Holland had, from time to time, petitioned the Holy See for the restoration of that Hierarchy without which the work of the Catholic Church in any country cannot be carried out in all its fulness. It was reserved for Pius IX. to confer upon them this favour.

In March, 1853, letters apostolical were sent to Holland appointing an archbishop and four bishops, and reconstructing that whole system of ecclesiastical government which had disappeared for so long a time. As was to have been expected, this act of spiritual jurisdiction met at first with the greatest opposition from those who were interested in the withholding religious liberty from their fellow-citizens. Thorbecke, the minister who, though a Protestant, had generously seconded the Dutch Catholics in this effort to obtain perfect freedom for their worship, was held up to execration as a "Jesuit in disguise."

The usual programme was followed out, but in this instance with not the least success.

By the month of June the act of the Pontiff received full and entire execution throughout Holland; and all

the woes and calamities predicted as a necessary consequence, were found to have no existence except, perhaps,
in the intellects of a few dangerous fanatics.

The restoration of these two hierarchies in England and
Holland ranks among the great facts of modern ecclesiastical history, and will always be mentioned among the
titles of Pius IX. to the gratitude of the Catholic Church.

This year (1853) was memorable also for the painful
differences which arose between the Sovereign Pontiff and
several Governments. The privilege of appointing to
vacant sees, which, under certain restrictions, had been
permitted to the Portuguese Government with regard to
their Eastern possessions, had been often abused, and for
a time altogether abandoned. In fact, this privilege,
vested in the hands of the Archbishop of Goa, had been
virtually resigned by not being made use of. Seeing this,
Pius IX., by the supremacy of spiritual power which
resides in him, took away from Goa the jurisdiction, and
himself appointed vicars-apostolic, to whom he committed
the care of this much-neglected people. A painful schism
followed, which the Portuguese Ministry, consisting
chiefly of infidels and Freemasons, did their utmost to
encourage and prolong. The clergy, however, in general
were faithful to the legitimate pastors, and the laity,
happily, followed the example set them by their priests;
and in the end the chief fomenter of all this misery, the
Bishop of Macao, who had been the very life of this
Eastern schism, submitted to the authority of the Church,
and gave the death-blow to the best hopes of those
opposed to it.

While the Goa difficulty was occupying the thoughts
and filling with grief the heart of the Sovereign Pontiff,

a painful dispute arose in the Duchy of Baden, between the Church and the civil authority. A Protestant Government, with a population almost three-fourths Catholic, nevertheless carried the spirit of intolerance to such a height as to endeavour to destroy the apostolic jurisdiction of the Catholic Bishops. Hermann, the noble Archbishop of Fribourg, was imprisoned, and his property seized, while the clergy were subjected to every kind of persecution short of bloodshed. The people, however, who had no idea of rendering to Cæsar "the things that were God's," rose in such opposition to the new oppressive measures, that the Government found itself compelled to deny its share in the acts of oppression that had taken place. With an unworthy equivocation, it declared that the seizure of the Church property was the work of the civil tribunals of the State, which were independent of their control. This was simply an unblushing falsehood, for the Government journals of the time had said, when the Archbishop was arrested, "Several events have compelled the Ministry to take these severe measures." But at all hazards the Government of Baden felt itself compelled to get out of the embarrassment into which it had so foolishly thrust itself, for all Catholic Germany sided as one man with the Archbishop. Austria, too, hinted very significantly that it might be dangerous for the question to remain much longer unsettled. So an amnesty was concluded between the Government and the Pontiff, which, in fact, was nothing less than a great triumph for the Church.

In the meantime the Chamber of Deputies at Turin continued that system of attack upon religion which, to far-seeing men, was a warning of what was to come.

Among other iniquitous measures, it voted the conscription of the clergy, and the further appropriation by the State of ecclesiastical property. It suppressed also the academy of Superga and the convent of Collegno, two foundations of the House of Savoy.

And King Victor Emmanuel looked on while in his name his Ministers contradicted the traditions of his pious race, and undid the work of his chivalrous ancestor.

Does it seem less than an act of retributive justice that he who has sullied the " white cross," no longer his own, should find himself at the present day stripped of that title which formed for ages the chief nobleness of the illustrious house from which he is descended? He has sold his birthright, and the home of his fathers, and the highest honour of an ancient, proud line, for the sake of French protection against the Austrian bayonets.

What has he gained by this act of domestic treachery? The honour of becoming the tool and the puppet of the revolutionary party! But he is neither King of Rome— for Pius IX. reigns in the capital of the Christian world —nor Duke of Savoy, for the "slopes of the Alps" were a "geographical necessity" for Louis Napoleon, and they now form part of the Empire of France.

We now come to an event in the pontificate of Pius IX. which by itself would suffice to hand down the memory of this Pope to the latest generations. We refer to the definition of the doctrine of the Immaculate Conception.

As early as 1849, whilst in exile, the Sovereign Pontiff had addressed himself to the bishops of the whole world, asking opinions and advice regarding this subject. The answers he received were such as to leave no doubt as to

M

what must have been the firm belief of the faithful in every age concerning the prerogatives of the Mother of God. Therefore, on the 8th of December, 1854, in the Sistine Chapel, in the presence of two hundred bishops and of the representatives of the whole world, the following decree was read aloud :

"That it is of faith that the ever Blessed Virgin Mary, from the first instant of her conception, by singular privilege and grace of God, by the merits of Jesus Christ, Saviour of the human race, was preserved and exempt from all stain of original sin."

This "definition" struck at several modern errors. It affirmed the truth of original sin, it established the fact of the fall of our first parents and the necessity of redemption, and of grace through Christ. As a consequence it struck at the fashionable modern heresy of the deification of man. It was also an expression of Papal Infallibility. It gave occasion for a new display of the power of Catholic unity, since the "ex cathedrâ" utterance of the Pontiff was at once everywhere accepted.

The Christian dogmas are immortal, like the God who has revealed them. They are neither inventions nor creations ; they are part of revelation, which the Church has power to define.

It may be permitted to the biographer to ask of the age in which he lives if it can possibly give an explanation of a most undeniable fact, namely, the ever-growing devotion to the Mother of God ? It has been called the phenomenon of our day. Christian cities place her statues in the great thoroughfares, and Christian soldiers wear her medal as a safety and a consolation through all the horrors of war. In fact, educated public opinion throughout Europe has agreed upon the reverence due to the Madonna.

Thus even the impious Polish poet Michiewitz knew that he was writing in accordance with the tastes of his readers when he put these words into the mouth of his hero, Conrad : " I know not wherein is my faith. I have nothing to do with the saints in the calendar; but I forbid you to blaspheme the holy name of Mary."

The *Concordat*, which was satisfactorily arranged at this time between the Pontiff and the Austrian Government, was a fact of immense importance to the interests of religion, inasmuch as it put an end to the state of things introduced by the Emperor Joseph II., and called from him, "Josephism."*

The disciples of Voltaire vehemently attacked this new measure, and, in doing this, they acted consistently, for they perfectly understood that the independence of the Church, and the full free action of religion amongst men tends more than anything else to establish firmly those thrones which they labour to pull down. However, their opposition was fruitless, except in keeping alive the spirit of antagonism against the Court of Rome, which now began to display itself as fiercely perhaps as ever.

In the English Parliament, the attacks upon the Papal Government were led by Earl Russell, and seconded by Lord Palmerston, the former, with characteristic bad

* Joseph II., named in contempt by Frederick II. " My brother the sacristan," was a relentless persecutor of the Church. At the hour of death, struck with remorse, he wrote for his epitaph these words :—" Here lies Joseph II., who was unhappy in all that he undertook."

M 2

taste, insulting France and Austria, by accusing them of having converted their protection of the Pontiff into a sovereignty; while the latter statesman, with his usual recklessness, asserted that the subjects of the Pope were in a state of barbarous ignorance, the country lying waste through neglect of the most ordinary tillage, etc.

The Exhibition which took place this year (1855) gave the most explicit contradiction to the statements made in the English House of Commons regarding the condition of the Papal States. The implements of Roman industry were marked with honourable distinction, while the samples of corn, etc., labelled "Roman," were the best proof that agriculture does not languish in the Patrimony.

While England speaks boastingly of her excellence in all that is material, and denounces the ignorance of countries which she imagines inferior to herself, the historians of the Continent assert (from our own statistics) that we are surrounded by thousands of our own countrymen who have scarcely yet heard of a Redeemer.

In poverty-stricken Rome, under the Pope, no man ever died from hunger; in wealthy London, within sight of the palaces of the great, death by famine is almost of weekly occurrence.

"But then, said the opponents of 'The Rule of the Monk,' the Campagna is so unhealthy, and the Pontine Marshes are not yet perfectly drained;" and with an admirable disdain for the facts of history and physical science, they urged this as a reason for yielding up Rome to the Piedmontese King. The indignant reply of the French satirist is the only one to be given here :—

"Why does not England banish her fogs, and (when he owned Savoy) why did not Victor Emmanuel cure cretinism* and pulverize Mont Blanc and the little St. Bernard?"

* A disease occasioned by the humid atmosphere, and the humid ground in the valleys of the Alps.

CHAPTER XXI.

The Congress of Paris — Cavour and the Papal Government — M. Rayneval and his Dispatch—English Debate of May, 1856— The Temporal Power—Granier de Cassagnac—Farini—The Tour of Pius IX. through his Dominions—Buon Campagni.

The first sitting of the Congress of Paris (25th February, 1856), which was held at the termination of the Crimean war, for the purpose of settling the "Eastern Question," was made use of by the revolutionary party at Turin as a means of introducing before the plenipotentiaries of Europe the subject of the Roman States in relation to the Government of Piedmont.

Sardinia, though only a fourth-rate power, by joining in the war against Russia, had obtained for the first time a sort of right to a place in the councils of the greater monarchies. Counts Cavour and Villamarina took care not to lose this opportunity of furthering the interests of their master, though at the expense of the rest of the Peninsula of Italy. A note, sent by these statesmen to Walewski, the French representative, and to Lord Clarendon, the plenipotentiary of England, expressed the great desirableness of separating the Legations * from the rule of the Sovereign Pontiff. This led to the consideration by a few of the members of the Congress of the then present condition of the Pontifical Government. With a coolness and audacity perhaps unrivalled in

* The "Legations" is the name for all the districts of the States of the Church, excepting Rome, Tivoli, and Subiaco.

Not content with the cession of Lombardy, from the Ticino to the Mincio, to which were added the Grand Duchy of Tuscany and the Duchies of Parma and Modena, Victor Emmanuel looked with a coveting eye upon the small but fair States of the Church. His agents, as we have already seen, had been long busy among the excitable Italian populations, urging them to revolt from their lawful sovereigns and to share in that glorious liberty which was to be universal, they said, whenever Piedmont should be supreme in the Peninsula.

In the Romagna * the Turin party had succeeded in obtaining what was called a popular vote in favour of annexation to Sardinia. We happen to be in possession of the explanation of the manner in which this " popular " vote was obtained; without such we confess the conduct of the Pope's subjects in 1859 and 1860, after the enthusiasm they displayed during the tour of 1857, would be perfectly inexplicable even from an Italian point of view. What, then, are the facts of the case with regard to the vote of the Romagnese, by which, it is said, the whole population implored Victor Emmanuel to receive them as a part of his happy dominion? In the first place, during the pretended voting in favour of annexation to Sardinia, liberty both of speech and of the press was strictly prohibited except to those who were known to be in the interest of Piedmont. Next, threats of assassination were of daily occurrence, in order to compel electors to vote for the annexation. The Marquis de Cabriac, in the Turin Chambers, did not hesitate to attribute the enormous deficit in the finances to the vast sums of money which

---

* A province of the Pope's dominions, bordering on the Adriatic, forty-five miles in length and thirty in breadth.

had been expended during the Romagna affair "upon electors and elected." Also, many of the most respectable citizens, consulting for their personal safety, left during the election, and their opinion was never recorded; whilst a large number of others, known for their loyalty to the Pontiff, found their names struck off the list of voters, and were told that their lives would not be safe if they ventured to remonstrate. Many, it is certain, abstained from voting altogether, "and this," says an Italian writer, "was the most that an honest man could do." The figures, it is true, appeared in the end to favour the ambition of Piedmont; but did they represent the wishes of the people?

Out of 18,000 electors in the province of Bologna, two-thirds recorded no vote at all!

At Rimini an amusing incident occurred. The number of the electors in this small town is 1200, yet 1800 votes were found by the assessors in the urn—"a great instance," says the author of the reply to the Romagnese memorandum, "of the danger of excessive zeal in one's friends." The same sort of absurd travestie of an election went on in the other towns, and the result was, that Europe was informed that Italy had chosen that her various States should be united into one undivided and constitutional sovereignty.

Nothing is easier than to carry any point if you possess power enough, and are sufficiently degraded to allow of no protest, how legitimate soever. Force has been the only argument employed by Piedmont in thus gaining from the Pontiff his richest provinces;—and for France (we should say, the French Government) to look on quietly at this act of violence was a solemn contradiction

which he should administer in the name of the Holy
See.

This insulting proposition was fortunately rejected by the
King of Sardinia, not certainly from any feeling of delicacy
regarding the feelings of the lawful prince, but simply
because he already aimed at something higher than the
position of steward and land agent to the Pontiff. His
emissaries, who were everywhere busy for him in the
Papal States, gave him the assurance that in a little while
all Italy would be his by the universal choice of the
different populations. So Victor Emmanuel informed his
good ally of France that he could not consent to accept
the honour which was sought to be put upon him.

But while these Christian monarchs were thus busy
legislating for the possessions of another, Pius IX. put
forth, in defence of his own right, a power which resides
nowhere but with the Chief Prince in Christendom.
This was an appeal to the people of the Catholic nations,
calling upon them to save their king and their father
from the destruction that was hanging over him both
from open enemies and false friends. It is said to have
been the thought of Merode, once himself a soldier, and
decorated on the field of battle by Bugeaud, to organize
a body of volunteers from every Christian state as a last
defence for the Pontiff against the revolutionary movements that were taking place unhindered, if not encouraged, by France throughout the Papal States. Roused
by the sublimity of the enterprize, the generous youth of
France and Belgium, and Germany and Holland (need
we add of Ireland?) hastened to the Eternal City. Lads
from college—in some instances boys from their mothers'

arms—young men from the midst of the ease of a life of
luxury, felt but one impulse—to rush to the help of that
feebleness which is sacred, of that royalty which is holy.
The matter-of-fact world was surprised to see that the
spirit of the nobleness of past Christian times was alive
still. The Catholic heroes who gathered round the
Pontiff to shield him from the daggers of assassins, and
to keep intact the patrimony of St. Peter, revived the
recollection of the age of chivalry. And they were not
left without a leader worthy of the cause in which they
were to perish. Far from the dissipation of Paris, in the
happiness of the bosom of his family, and surrounded by
friends, " the Zouave maker," the conqueror of Africa,
and the deliverer of France from the horrors of Communism, General Lamoricière received an invitation from
Pius IX. to become his soldier. It could hardly have
been that the Bayard of modern Christendom should
refuse. Indeed he at once joyously accepted the dignity,
exclaiming, "This is a cause for which one may be proud
to die."

To a friend who endeavoured to dissuade him from the
enterprize he answered : "I know all the perils of the
case, but when the chief of the Church calls upon any
one of his children to defend him hesitation would be a
crime. I shall go to Rome and shall defend the Pope,
since no one else is willing. I will die there if necessary."

"It was," wrote Montalembert, "not only sacrifice of
life, but of name, reputation, military glory, ancient vic-
tories. He knew what was in store for him in a worldly
point of view, yet at once, as formerly at the siege of
Constantine, he threw himself headlong into the breach."

"You have never yet been conquered," said one of his companions, "but you will be now."

"The cause is worth it all," replied the hero.

"But they will say you are no longer a Frenchman."

"My friend," said Lamoricière, "when I die I shall not be asked if I knew the penal code, but my catechism; and before opening the gates of Paradise they will not examine whether those of my country have been shut against me."

In a letter which the world has read he wrote thus: "If they in France (meaning the Emperor) take from me my rank as French citizen, the Catholic world will restore it to me by acclamation."

On the 19th of March, 1860, he wrote to his old friend Bedeau these words in regard to the new duty he had taken up: "I have no hope but in God; human strength cannot achieve what I am trying to effect. It is not boldness but devotedness, the reward of which I expect above—most assuredly not here."

Joined to Lamoricière in the service of the Pontiff was another hero, with an unblemished character, the young Count George de Pimodan, whose heroic wife said to him: "Go, and you will make your sword glorious."

The Count de Pimodan was a soldier worthy to have fought at the side of St. Louis the Crusader, the very soul of chivalry, "a perfect gentle knight." After the battle of Castatoria he purchased from his men the golden medals which they had taken from the necks of the slain. "They are pledges," said he, "from pious mothers and fond sisters and wives to the brave men whom they will never see again. Let us leave them on the hearts of the valiant dead."

Great was the rage of the revolutionists of Europe to see the first soldier of the first army in the world standing by the side of the Sovereign Pontiff.

From the Thames to the Arno rose a cry of disappointment and execration. Yet they were soon to be consoled, for the soldiers of the faith were doomed to be betrayed.

Farini and Cialdini, with sixty thousand men, were to secure a doubtful victory over about five thousand; and they who would have annihilated the bands from Tuscany and Lombardy were overwhelmed by the whole army of Sardinia.

As he had expected, Lamoricière found all the defences of the Pontifical States in the worst possible condition.

Even after a labour of months at reconstruction, in his letter to the Emperor of Austria he writes: "I have in all sixteen battalions. The garrison of Ancona takes two of these; of the rest, twenty companies are required to garrison the fortified towns. Waggon trains I have none. Only one of the battalions is armed with the Minié rifle. The drivers of the artillery are altogether inexperienced. The French arsenal is put at the disposal of the Piedmontese, whilst I am refused permission even to purchase arms in France."

At the end of October Lamoricière received a letter from Fanti, the Piedmontese general in Romagna, to the effect that he would occupy Umbria and the Marches if the Papal troops attempted to "repress the national spirit."

The answer to this was the following dispatch from the Minister of War: "The French embassy at Rome has been informed that the Emperor Napoleon has written to the King of Piedmont (sic) declaring that if the latter attacked the Papal States, *he would be opposed by force.*"

The excuse that has been attempted to be made for the treachery displayed towards the Pontiff after this solemn declaration that "force" would be used in his favour by France, displays either the grossest ignorance of the facts of the case or else the most unblushing effrontery in the face of them. For instance, it has been said that the words in the dispatch, *colla forza* (with force), meant only that the French Emperor would employ moral force, such as the interference of the Ministry, &c., if Piedmont should attack the Pope.

Unfortunately for this explanation of a great baseness, we happen to possess another telegram sent by the Duke de Grammont to the consul at Ancona, and in every sense an official document. It is in the following words:—
"If the Piedmontese troops penetrate into the Pontifical territory, the Emperor will be obliged to oppose them. Orders have been given to embark troops at Toulon, and these reinforcements will arrive immediately. The Government of the Emperor will not tolerate the culpable aggression of the Sardinian Government."

Would the moral force explanation suffice for this telegram in the mind of any reasonable being?

Following quickly on the letter of General Fanti to Lamoricière went a dispatch from Cavour to Cardinal Antonelli, couched in these insolent terms:—Sardinia will invade the Papal States unless the Pope shall disband his "mercenaries." Even the *Times* newspaper was compelled to call this "a novel and a startling policy."

Antonelli's answer was worthy his rank, as the first

statesman in Europe:—"The disorder in our States comes from yourself and your agents; your invitation to disarm is accompanied by a menace, which I abstain from qualifying. The Holy See appeals to the law of nations, and against your violence it is my duty to protest energetically in the name of his Holiness."

Another curt note from the Piedmontese general to Lamoricière, containing only these words:—"Dismiss your mercenaries;" and before any answer could be returned, Fanti, Cialdini and Rocca, with 60,000 men, crossed the boundary. The little army of Pope Pius retreated upon Ancona, while Cialdini occupied the heights of Castelfidardo, and pushed on as far as le Brocetti.

CHAPTER XXVI.

On the hills of Loretto, at the foot of that sanctuary which Christendom reverences, the small band of Catholic warriors encamped on the night of the 15th of September.

They were already sealed for death in defence of the Church.

To use the words of the pious Duchess of Parma, "they were ready to die for a saint led on by a hero." In fact they were about to throw away their lives in vindication of the patrimony of St. Peter, and to give an admirable example to the world of the devotedness of faith.

The proclamation issued by their leader was worthy of them and their cause: "We fight for that which is the principle of the life of Christianity. The Revolution, like Islamism formerly, threatens Europe to-day; and to-day, therefore, as in former times, the Pope's cause is that of civilization and of the liberty of the world."

On the 16th Lamoricière descended the heights of Monte Santo, defeating the Sardinian outposts and driving them in disorder into the town. By the evening of the 18th, having been joined by De Pimodan with 2500 men, he was able to concentrate 8000 troops at the little town of Loretto. Finding himself hemmed in on all sides by the entire army of Piedmont, with no hopes of safety, except by cutting his way through the enemy to Ancona, he resolved, with that desperation which had won for him already many a victory, to attempt next day the deadly task.

The evening previous to the battle was spent by the soldiers of Pius in all the exercises of devotion.

The priests who accompanied the troops were busy until far into the night with the sacred duty of confessing and absolving these gallant few, thus fitting them for the fate of the morrow.

With the earliest dawn the men stood ready at their posts, the dome of the "holy house," that majestically crowns the heights, glittering above them in the rising sun.

Caillard, a young priest of Angers, turning to them, said : " Gentlemen, you have the honour of fighting for the Church. Show yourselves worthy of this. God asks from each of you now one thought of love, one act of repentance, for I am about to give you the Divine blessing."

The orders were that they should rush upon Loretto, which was occupied by the enemy, and endeavour to effect by surprise what would be otherwise an impossibility with their inferior numbers. They were led to this desperate attack by the Counts de Pimodan and Bourbon.

The latter said : " Comrades, we are about to die that others may gain by it ; " while the former, drawing his sword, and pointing in the direction of the enemy, cried out, "Remember that you are Frenchmen and Catholics."

The men shared the enthusiasm of their officers, and, their best blood thus roused, fell upon the troops of Piedmont with an irresistible fury. The latter fled, after a short resistance, and sought protection in the support of their main body. Again and again, with thinned ranks and exhausted strength, did the soldiers of the Pontiff beat back the overwhelming odds by which they were encountered.

It was in vain; the whole Sardinian army was at hand, and fresh troops by thousands were pouring in to reinforce their comrades. Wearied with slaughter, his ammunition well-nigh expended and left almost without officers, Lamoricière saw at a glance that there was but one hope left.

Collecting together the shattered relics of his small force, he put himself at their head and, with that terrible impetuosity which had won Africa for France, he swept a pathway for himself and his followers through the serried ranks of the enemy, and reached in a few hours the town of Ancona, which was still held by Pontifical troops.

Thus ended the battle of Castelfidardo, in which 45,000 men, well provided with arms of precision and parks of artillery, fought for hours against about 8000 volunteers, with very doubtful success.

The Count de Pimodan fell early in the action.

Wounded in three places, he said to the men who carried him from the battle-field, "Let me die here; return to your posts." He lingered in great agony long enough to hear of the defeat of the Pontifical army and

the retreat of Lamoricière. Raising himself with difficulty at the sad tidings, he exclaimed, "But the cause is
not yet lost," and falling back he expired.

The hero was right. The independence of the Church
was not decided at the massacre of Castelfidardo ; and
men never die for the Church without hope.

"It is an established law," says Bossuet, "that the
Church gains no advantage that does not cost the lives of
some of her children. To defend her rights she must shed
her blood." The death of all who fight for her and with
her is never loss.

"Her soldiers," says an eloquent writer, "do not stay
to discuss how they are to reconcile the gift of Pepin and
Charlemagne with modern ideas. They say the Vicar of
Christ on earth is a king, and shall be such ; it is for this
royalty they fight."

Neither will the world be ever able to exhaust the
recruits that will for ever reinforce this army, for you
must strike dead the heart of the Catholic world before
you can destroy the Pontiff; and so long as the faith
shall burn within a single breast, the successor of St.
Peter shall have at least one champion.*

* The Count de Pimodan lies buried in the Church of St. Louis, by
the wish of Pius IX., who himself wrote the inscription for his tomb.
We are only too conscious how much this beautiful epitaph suffers in
translation:—

TO

GEORGE PIMODAN,

THE MOST NOBLE AND COURAGEOUS CHIEFTAIN,

WHO, RECKLESS OF LIFE,

DIED FOR THE HOLY APOSTOLIC SEE

LAMENTED BY THE CATHOLIC WORLD,

THE SOVEREIGN PONTIFF, PIUS IX.,

IN HIS OWN NAME, AND THAT OF THE ROMAN CHURCH,

HATH RENDERED WEEPING THE FUNERAL HONOURS

DUE TO SUCH COURAGE AND PIETY.

Lamoricière has been blamed for the rash sacrifice of life of which he was the cause at Castelfidardo, by fighting when he must have known that success was impossible. But is this accusation just? Had he not received assurances both from France and Austria?

He knew that within easy reach there was an army of the very men he had trained to warfare, before whose line of battle the troops of Sardinia would have been little better than a handful of dust. And he held an official promise of the aid of these. It was not his fault that the knightly honour of St. Louis was lightly esteemed by the ruler of France.

The object of Lamoricière in fighting at Castelfidardo was that he might be able to reach Ancona, where he reasonably concluded his presence would encourage every supporter of Pope Pius. The place he knew was sufficiently strong for him to hold out until the arrival of Guyon, with the French division, and the Archduke Maximilian, with the Austrian fleet.

He put "his trust in princes," and they betrayed him and the cause of the Church—the one for the sake of the sweetness of revenge, and the other from motives of worldly policy.

In the meanwhile, Lamoricière, having succeeded in reaching Ancona, prepared to hold this place to the last extremity, still hoping that some of the succour which had been so solemnly promised might arrive before it was too late.

He was to be again disappointed. Ancona, speedily invested by sea and land, with 50,000 men guarding the blockade, and 400 guns pouring destruction and death into its streets and dwellings, was defended by him with

4000 men till the last cartridge was fired away. Hour
after hour during the siege did this noble soldier
cast an anxious hopeful eye across the Adriatic, watching
for that help which was not to come. That he had a
right to expect it, and therefore was justified in the fierce
defence which he offered to the entire armament of Sardinia, is evident from facts which have since come to
light.

It is now certain that the division of the army of the
Mincio was ready to start to the relief of Ancona, that the
order to this effect was signed when the evil advisers of
Francis Joseph interfered, and by their arguments of fear
and prudence altered the whole face of things, and robbed
their master of a surpassing glory. "The wounds of
Solferino and Magenta are not yet healed," said they;
"if you act in this cause of the Pope, France will cross
the Alps, the revolutionists will rise again, and all will
be lost."

The reply of the Austrian Emperor was worthy of a
Catholic prince. "If my throne is to be destroyed,"
he said, "I should prefer to lose it in the Marches of the
Vatican than at the gates of Vienna." However, he
suffered himself to be overruled, and saved that army,
which might have brought triumph to the cause of the
Church, only to be afterwards annihilated by Prussia at
Sadowa.

Deserted and betrayed on all sides, Lamoricière surrendered Ancona, with all the honours of war. Arriving
at Rome, he was received by Pius IX. as his son, while
the Roman magistracy gave him the patrician rank.
Indignant France displayed her feelings by voting him a
sword. At Paris, Marseilles, and Lyons, his reception

was like a triumph. "Not one of my ancient comrades has disowned me," exclaimed the grateful warrior, overwhelmed with the sympathy and admiration that greeted him everywhere.

The only act of the French Government towards carrying out its solemn promise, that Sardinia should be resisted "by force," had been the withdrawal of its ambassador from Turin !

The contest being thus ended, the King of Piedmont issued a proclamation, in which he attempted to justify his occupation of the Pontifical territory.

The opinion passed upon his act of spoliation by the *Times* may be taken as being that of Europe generally. "Victor Emmanuel has in Garibaldi a most formidable opponent. He must, therefore, revolutionize the Papal States in order to arrest the revolutionary movement at home. Self-preservation has superseded all other considerations. Whilst holding out assurances of respect and reverence for the chief of the Church, Victor Emmanuel speaks of the Pope in terms of bitterness and acrimony unusual in the present age, even in a declaration of war."

There now remained to Pius IX. not a single soldier either in Umbria or the Marches. From a human point of view the cause was lost. But firm faith still asked this question, "Shall Turin and its renegade prince be able to overthrow that providential law which drove Otho, and Barbarossa, and Napoleon the Great, far from Rome ? "

P

CHAPTER XXVII.

Victor Emmanuel declared "King of all Italy"—The protest of Pius IX.—The *Times* upon the act of Sardinia—The deceitful language of Louis Napoleon and Victor Emmanuel—Ricasoli and Montalembert—The spoiler disappointed—Garibaldi, the last hope of the Republicans—His address to Hungary, and Klapka's reply—The Cabinet of Turin in a difficulty—It denounces Garibaldi as a Rebel—Aspromonte, a strange spectacle—" Et tu Brute ! "

The Turin Parliament, which met in February, 1861, began its work by an official declaration that Victor Emmanuel was prince and king over all Italy.

To those who believe in the immoral doctrine that accomplished facts confer rights, this title which the son of Charles Albert assumed was in a measure consistent. To others, who still hold the antiquated and unfashionable theory that successful physical strength upon the side of injustice can never change that injustice into lawfulness, the assumption by Victor Emmanuel of the title of the King of all Italy merely added to the guilt of that violence and [fraud which had for a time triumphed over right.

So thought Pius IX.; and therefore, in his name, wrote Antonelli to the foreign ambassadors at Rome in these words, ["A Catholic king, forgetful of every religious principle, having little by little despoiled the august head of the] Church of the most flourishing part of his legitimate possessions, has now entitled himself King of Italy. . . . . The Holy Father puts forth a fresh protest against the assumption of a title tending to legitimatize the iniquity of so many facts. . . . . The title arrogated by the King of Sardinia is an injury to justice, and to the sacred property of the Church, and will never be recognized by the Holy Father."

Thus spoke the Pontiff, pleading his own cause and that of the dethroned princes of the Peninsula, and at the same time denouncing the modern doctrine that. the strongest is the most lawful possessor.

Others, too, by no means friendly to the Pope's cause, were fair enough to acknowledge that the act of Sardinia was simply brigandage. "Victor Emmanuel," said the *Times* of March, 1861, "took part in the Russian war without being a party to any treaty relating to the Sublime Porte. He next took advantage of a popular commotion to annex Tuscany and the Legations, although neither the Grand Duke nor the Pope had any part in the war of 1859. Sardinia has invaded the States of the Pontiff without any declaration of war and under futile pretexts. She has connived with Garibaldi, and has profited by his audacity."

Whilst the underhand political intrigue of Napoleon and Victor Emmanuel was working out successfully their highest hopes, what was the language of "these perjured kings and dishonoured gentlemen"?

At the very moment that Cialdini was receiving orders to attack Lamoricière and to seize the dominions of the Pontiff the King of Sardinia wrote: "I wish always to respect the See of the Chief of the Church, and to give him all the guarantees of independence and surety."

On the day before the battle at Castelfidardo the message forwarded to the French Government by Victor Emmanuel was the following, which we can almost

excuse the reader if he should call in question : "We
enter the Marches and Umbria to establish order without
touching the authority of the Pope, and to give battle,
if necessary, to the Revolution on the Neapolitan territory."

So it was for moral order, for the sake of peace, to
render secure the Pontifical throne, and to destroy the
Revolution, that Sardinia sent Cialdini to massacre the
Pope's troops and to seize the provinces of the Church !
It was "to give battle to the Revolution on the
Neapolitan territory" that Victor Emmanuel carried
out exactly the revolutionary programme in the Papal
States !

The cool impudence which could put forward such a
statement could be equalled only by the credulity that
could accept it.

The language used by the ally of Piedmont in the
spoliation of the Pontiff was not less remarkable. Thus :
"The Emperor will continue, with that perseverance
which Europe honours, to defend the just interests of
France, the independence of the Holy Father, and the
liberty of Italy."

Twenty days after the above sentence was written
Billault, replying to Jules Favre, the orator of the
Revolution, said officially in the French Senate: "To
abandon the policy which France has followed for ages,
to forget that the Pope has for ten years been defended
by us at Rome, is impossible." Barthe also said, speaking
for the Government: "The Pope is the principle
representative of moral force in the world, and must
be maintained."

But Victor Emmanuel had set his heart on Rome.

The contest was, however, exceedingly brief, and Garibaldi and his son Menotti were wounded and made prisoners.

To be struck down by an Italian bullet, to be crippled for life and by his own party ought to have sufficed to open the eyes of this brave fanatic to the sort of principles governing the conduct of that party which, for years, has made him its convenient tool. One of the foremost to place the crown of Naples and Sicily upon the head of Victor Emmanuel : all he received was a gratitude truly Italian.

When his followers were dispersed, and he himself incapable of doing harm any longer, the Cabinet of Ratazzi generously forgave him for having followed its own instructions, and rewarded his devotedness to the cause which his sovereign had most at heart by the sentence of banishment !

CHAPTER XXVIII.

From the end of the year 1862 until the December of 1866, Pius IX. enjoyed in his curtailed dominions an external peace.

But during the whole of this period both Victor Emmanuel and the French Emperor were busy, each endeavouring to solve the "Roman Question," regardless in their manner of doing it of the feelings of the chief person concerned. The object of the King of Piedmont was grossly evident, viz., the "possession of all Italy, and of the capital of the Christian world;" while to Napoleon the best interests of worldly policy seemed to require that he should as speedily as possible evacuate Rome, respect being simulated all the while of the removal of his troops, for the naturally strong feeling upon this subject of the great Catholic people over whom he ruled.

It was during the course of the secret diplomacy between France and Italy upon the subject of Rome and the Pontiff, that Europe was startled by a new difficulty. Stung into madness by the atrocities of her savage conqueror, Poland had once more risen in arms.

Upon that brief but terrible effort, made by a brave Christian people to regain the rights of common humanity, it is no part of our present duty to dwell, except so far as it gave occasion for the display of those qualities in the Sovereign Pontiff which have served more than temporal power and earthly magnificence to bind the heart of the Christian to him and to his office.

England, called "The Home of the Free," had in many different ways urged on the Poles to rise in insurrection against their tyrant, and had substantially aided them in their aspirations after freedom. Yet, it is certain that one short note received from Count Bismarck, on the part of Prussia, was sufficient to induce us to leave Poland to her fate. France, in the meanwhile, thought that barren sympathy was ample payment of her great debt to this gallant nation; while, to her eternal shame, Italy forwarded to the Russian despot, by the hands of Pepoli, the revolutionist, a letter of condolence, in which the revolt and its authors and abettors are stigmatized in language that must find a warm response in every tyrant's heart.

Such is the love of legitimate liberty taught in the school of the revolution.

How did Pius IX. act?

He addressed two letters to the Czar of Russia, unequalled for the Christian courage in which they denounce the atrocities of the latter, demanding of him, in the name of humanity and under threat of the severest judgment of God, that he should abstain from a policy which the law of nature condemned, and which religion held accursed.

In July, 1863, Cardinal Reisach was sent by the Pontiff to Vienna, to insist that Austria should do her utmost to defend "the Christian people of Poland" from the fury of the Russian Government; and in the September of the same year prayers were ordered throughout the world by the same Power for Poland, "That ancient bulwark of Christendom."

Thus, alone of all the sovereigns of Europe, in every age of Christianity, has the Supreme Pontiff defended the weak and the oppressed, and has maintained with a courage that no menace could daunt the eternal obligation of right. In this way have the Popes proved themselves the preservers of society and the world.

That right is absolute, and that accomplished facts, when they are the result of fraud and violence, have no authority over obedience is the highest teaching of all law worthy of the name. This is the great rule that the Popes, with a marvellous traditional tenacity, have laboured to impress upon the conscience of Europe. Whenever they have failed in this legitimate purpose the explanation of their want of success will be found in their comparatively feeble condition as earthly princes. Had they power, as they have right, to enforce morality, the oppression of one class by the other would be unheard of throughout the nations of Christendom.

The year which followed the uprising of Poland was remarkable in Italy for two events: the removal of the capital of Piedmont to Florence from Turin (a change not effected without bloodshed); and for the convention entered into between France and Sardinia with regard to the position of the Sovereign Pontiff.

This Convention of September, 1864, which was negociated by Pepoli on the part of Sardinia, and by Drouyn de Lhuys on that of France, stipulated as follows:—1. That Sardinia should not attack the present territory of the Holy Father, and should also resist by force any attack from without. 2. That the French Emperor should withdraw his troops gradually, in proportion as the army which the Pontiff was to raise should be organized and placed upon a war footing. The entire evacuation by France to be completed in two years at the latest. 3. The Government of Victor Emmanuel to raise no protest against a volunteer army for the defence of the Pope, no matter how composed.

"We are resolved not to abandon this post of honour until the object of our occupation has been obtained."

Thus wrote Drouyn de Lhuys to the French Ambassador at Rome only three days before signing the Convention with Sardinia, which was, on the part of the French Government, a deliberate yielding up of the Pope into the hands of his worst enemy.

As to the assurance given by Sardinia, neither to invade nor suffer the invasion of the Papal States, her after conduct proved that her solemn promise on this occasion was not worth the paper upon which it was expressed.

Was Louis Napoleon ignorant of the morality of his ally? Could he not have suspected that the restraining clauses of the Convention would be powerless so soon as the last French soldier was out of sight of the walls of Rome? Or did he secretly desire that, having fulfilled on his part what seemed all the exactions of modern honour, Victor Emmanuel might find himself with nothing between his ambition and its fulfilment, save that which he has habitually disregarded, namely, his kingly word?

The contracting parties to this convention cleverly kept

their deliberations a secret from the Pontiff. The latter did not hear of the decisions of the convention until thirteen days after all was concluded.

However much he must have felt this desertion of his cause by the Emperor, Pius IX. had too princely a soul to stoop to remonstrance or entreaty. With an energy that has never yet shown itself unequal to any calamity, he set to work to organize a little army for his defence against those who have taught him that they respect nothing but force.

The small band of heroes who gathered once more at the Pontiff's call were worthy successors of the men of Castelfidardo, and ready for such another sacrifice.

All nations of Christendom sent volunteers for this service—for the children of faith dwell everywhere; there is no corner of the earth in which men are not to be found who regard the Pope as spiritual king and father : and this fact alone shows how utterly inapplicable is the phrase, "hired mercenaries," which General Cialdini (and after him the London press) has applied to the soldiers of Pius IX. If the flower of the patrician blood of France, and Belgium, and Spain, is to be so designated, what name shall be given to the Garibaldian legion, which it is notorious was made up of " area sneaks " from Bloomsbury, pickpockets from the Borough, billiard-sharpers from Baden-Baden, and the sweepings of the gaols of all the great cities of Europe.

True to her traditions, Catholic France sent a whole legion of volunteers to guard the Pontiff's throne when the regular army should be withdrawn by the Emperor's Government. It took its name from that old town of Provence which, backed by the maritime Alps, and fortified by the science of Vauban, presents an impregnable barrier for France on the side of Italy.

If, in the battle of Mentana (soon to be fought), the Chassepot rifle of the regulars "did wonders," it was not, however, before the men of the "Antibes Legion" had routed the choicest troops of the Revolution.

The close of the year 1866 was a time of great excitement in Rome.

That army, which for seventeen years had held the post of honour in the Eternal City, heard with regret and indignation the order for its return to France. From the commander-in-chief to the lowest drummer-boy it was felt as a humiliation, as an unchivalrous abandonment.

During the long period of the occupation, Pius IX., by a thousand acts of courtesy and sweetness, in which the dignity of the prince had only served to illustrate the sublime affection of the priest, had won the hearts alike of men and officers. To leave him with such a power as Sardinia at his gates seemed to them little else than a base betrayal. And when, on that well-remembered December morning, the Pope, his voice tremulous with emotion, gave his blessing to the troops before their departure, and said, "The French soldier has imperishable claims to my gratitude," exclamations of sorrow, of anger, and of shame rose on all sides, more in harmony with the soul of St. Louis than with that of Louis Napoleon.

Replying to the address presented by the French officers, Pius IX. said: "It is idle to deceive ourselves; the Revolution will come. A person high in position has already said, 'Italy is made, but not completed.' He would feel undone if there yet remained a single corner

of the earth here in a state of order and justice. Six
years ago I said to your Emperor : 'St. Augustine,
Bishop of Hippo (now part of the French Empire),
affrighted at the ruin that the barbarians were
occasioning in his diocese, prayed that he might die
and not witness it.' The reply I received was, 'The
barbarians will not come to you.' He has not been
a true prophet. I fear the Revolution. But what can
I do? What can I say? I am without resources. But
I am calm, for the Almighty God gives me constancy.
And now receive my blessing. If you should see the
Emperor of the French, tell him I pray for him. As
for me, I live in the mercy of God."

"Time and the course of events will now solve the
Roman Question," exclaimed Victor Emmanuel, when
informed of what had taken place.

He was soon to witness a solution of it that he
had not quite expected.

CHAPTER XXIX.

The war of 1866, between Italy and Prussia, combined against Austria, although by the intervention of the French Emperor it ended in the aggrandizement of the kingdom of Victor Emmanuel, still, in its details, proved that had Italy stood alone it would certainly have been crushed by the House of Hapsburg.

Whenever, during the campaign, the army of Italy met that of Austria on an equal footing, defeat of the former seemed to follow as a matter of course.

At Custozza the rout was so complete that the fugitives only saved themselves from complete destruction by a precipitate retreat across the Mincio, while in the naval combat off the Island of Lissa the wooden vessels of Austria sank and scattered the ironclads of Sardinia. Admiral Persano thought it no small achievement to be able to reach Ancona with a few shattered hulks.

We allude to these facts, which do not belong to our subject, for the sake of making it clear that Pius IX. was not the infatuated being his enemies wish it to be supposed in the assurance he entertained that his own volunteer army ought to be, and would be, if rightly

Q

handled, more than a match for the Italian invader. It could hardly be expecting too much to hope that men from France and Ireland, from Belgium and Spain, should be at least the equals of those who fled before the Croats trained by Benedick.

As we shall soon see, the Pontiff's judgment of the quality of his troops was the correct one.

The year 1866 closed with the appearance of two documents, which we venture to place before the reader, and which, when compared with events soon to occur, will enable him to form a correct opinion of the honour of the Piedmontese King and his ministers.

The circular issued by Ricasoli in November, 1866, and addressed to the prefects of the kingdom, was in these words: "The Roman Question remains unsolved, but after the fulfilment of the September Convention that question cannot and must not be a motive for agitation. The sovereignty of the Pope is placed by the Convention of September in the position of all other sovereignties. Italy has promised France and Europe to remain neutral between the Pope and the Romans. . . . , Italy must keep her promise. . . . . All agitation having for pretext the "Roman Question" must therefore be discountenanced, prevented and repressed. . . . . The Italian Government does not desire to lessen the independence of the Chief of Catholicity."

Following this, came the words of Victor Emmanuel himself, on December 15th: "The French Government, faithful to the obligations of the September Convention, has withdrawn its troops from Rome. On its side, the Italian Government, observant of its engagements, has respected, and will respect, the Pontifical territory. . . . .

bidding of the Revolution to achieve another triumph like that of Castelfiardo, went like an electric shock. The French people rose as one body against the repetition of any such dishonour to the national flag.

The small opposition of the minority, called in derision the "Piedmontese of Paris," served only to make more clear to the Emperor that to adhere to the cause which he had always secretly cherished, for which in his youth he had fought, would be, in fact, to risk his own sovereignty, and the removal of his dynasty from the throne of France.

He was not the man to hesitate at such a crisis. The defence of Pius IX. was at once entered upon with all the fervour of the most devoted Ultramontanist. Never was witnessed so rapid a change in the policy of a Government. No praise was too high for the Pope and his supporters; no language too severe or too threatening for his enemies.

Italy had broken the Convention; it was a point of honour, therefore, for France to intervene. Victor Emmanuel was unable or unwilling to protect the Sovereign Pontiff against invasion from without. In either case the duty devolved upon France. The French people were resolved that the "gesta Dei per Francos" should not be omitted in those days, etc.

Deeds soon followed such words; and before men had recovered from their surprise at the suddenness of the Imperial conversion the armament from Toulon was on its way to Italy.

In the meanwhile swarms of volunteers still crossed the frontier, and established themselves, after several slight skirmishes, on the Pontifical territory. They were headed by Menotti Garibaldi, who established his head-quarters at Nerola.

On the 13th of October, 1867, the Papal troops defeated a body of the insurgents on the road to Monte Libretto ; but in attempting to take Nerola, where the insurgents were massed in great force, the Zouaves (called by the Garibaldians "devils of the good God ") were beaten with great loss, and retreated to Monte Maggiore.

At this juncture the "hermit of Caprera," in spite of the guard that surrounded his island (or, as some assert, assisted by this very guard), succeeded in effecting his escape, reached the mainland, and appeared once more in the midst of the insurrectionists.

It will indeed be a difficult task for the Cabinet of Florence to clear itself (if it should ever desire to do so) of its complicity in this dishonourable affair. As to the positive sanction giving afterwards to the acts of Garibaldi there is no longer any question. It is certain that at Genoa Garibaldi published to the world that he was about to march upon Rome. At Florence he had a long conference with the Minister Ratazzi, and after-wards harangued his followers in front of the king's palace ; and then set out in a special train for the seat of war ! Where was the honour of Italy's king all this while ? But with France hastening to the scene of action, no other power was wanted.

At the end of October Garibaldi succeeded in capturing Monte Rotondo, which is not far from Rome. The little town was gallantly defended, by about 350 Papal Zouaves, for twenty-seven hours, against a force ten times their number. They yielded only after the fifth assault, having first succeeded in spiking their cannon.

On taking possession of this place, the revolutionists carried out their usual programme. The church was pillaged, pictures and images destroyed, the organ burnt, and the valuable windows of stained glass fired at for amusement. The inhabitants also were plundered of everything that could be forced from them by threats of instant death. Here Garibaldi established his camp, while General Kanzler, the Commander-in-Chief of the Pontifical troops, withdrew all his men from the provinces, except the garrisons at Civita Vecchia and Viterbo, and concentrated them on Rome.

But now at length they were at hand before whom the openly avowed freebooter, as well as his royal supporter, would be equally impotent. With a far-seeing prudence, which some have stigmatized as cowardice, Victor Emmanuel was already beginning the humiliating task of soothing the anger of his Imperial keeper.

The unfortunate and ill-used Garibaldi was the first to be sacrificed to the necessities of his sovereign's policy. It was on the 25th of October that a circular of Moustier, French Minister of Foreign Affairs, appeared, addressed to the diplomatic agents of France, and explaining the cause of the new intervention in Italy, on the part of the Emperor. Only two days after this, and little more than a week after Garibaldi had received assurances not only of impunity, but of real aid, came a proclamation of Victor Emmanuel against the Garibaldians and their leader, in which an awkward attempt was made to propitiate Louis Napoleon. "A war," it said, "between France and Italy would be fratricidal." With more truth it could have stated that such a war would have been for Italy annihilation.

On the 28th the French fleet was off Civita Vecchia. On the 30th the troops of the "Grande Nation" were parading the streets of Rome. No time was to be lost if the Revolution was to be crushed without farther complications, for it was very much to be feared that if unoccupied, the French soldier might, in his present temper, regard (and naturally) the army of Victor Emmanuel, which was then at last, when not required, making its appearance, as the real enemy, and might act accordingly.* It was, therefore, resolved to attack Garibaldi at once, in his position at Monte Rotondo, near Mentana.

On the 2nd of November General Kanzler, with the Count de Courteau, at the head of 3000 Pontifical troops, and accompanied by a French column under Baron de Polhès, left Rome by the Porta Pia and took the direction of the headquarters of the enemy.

The two armies met at Mentana, and, to use the words of the official dispatch, "after four hours' fighting, night prevented the complete success of the Papal Zouaves; at daybreak the second column was ready to renew the combat, but the Garibaldians exhibited a flag of truce." Baron Polhès, the French commander, said of the battle of Mentana: "It was a small Solferino; this one word will convey my impression of the bravery of the Pontifical troops."

The Garibaldians surrendered at discretion, and met with a generosity from the victors which they themselves had never practised. Amongst the slain were found many of the soldiers of Victor Emmanuel provided with billets

---

* We have the officer's report upon this point, stating that the danger of a collision between the troops of France and Sardinia was most imminent.

containing these words: "The bearer has unlimitted leave of absence."

"Comment, in order to understand this," says a French writer, "is quite unnecessary."

Garibaldi escaped from the capitulation, but was arrested soon afterwards and imprisoned at Varignano, on the Gulph of Spezzia.

The debate in the French Chambers that followed upon the failure of the conspirators was evidence of the present hopelessness of the revolutionary cause. Never had the Catholic party spoken with such confidence and such contempt. It resembled in many points the great oratorical struggle of October, 1849, but it wanted its strong element of opposition. The Emperor lead the way in these words: "The Convention of September, 1864, not having been executed, I have been compelled once again to send our troops to Rome, and to protect the power of the Holy See, by repulsing the invaders."

He was followed by Baron Dupin, who, after thanking the Government for rescuing the Pontiff, said: "France has one resource, that is, Catholicity. Is not the French Government the natural defender of this religion of two hundred millions? It cannot fail in this mission, and in fulfilling it the Emperor will make of France the first Power in the world."

The Cardinal Archbishop of Rouen, on the same subject, said: "The whole series of acts of the Italian Government leave no room to doubt that Italy wishes to complete her unity in absorbing Rome. . . . Italian unity disputes in the face of Europe the right of the temporal Papacy to live on Italian soil. Italian unity is the work of secret conspirators, of fraud, corruption,

intimidation and crime. The Government of Florence
has trampled on the most sacred engagements, and
sooner or later will become the victim of the passions it
has evoked. . . . God grant that this Russia of the
South may not become a peril for us. . . . I know that
some say the Pope can remain free in the Vatican, while
Victor Emmanuel and his Parliament sit in the Capitol.
The Catholic world will never accept these terms—will
never endure that St. Peter's successor should be at the
mercy of a Cavour. What, then, are we to do ? I do
not ask you to give the death-blow yourselves to this
kingdom of Italy, since you have willed its existence.
But as this new power declares itself incompatible with
that which constitutes the life of the moral world of the
universe, let us await the disposition of Providence; let
us allow that to crumble to pieces which is destined to
perish, and let us remain the defenders of that which
cannot fail."

"A king of Italy," said the Archbishop of Paris, " is
too paltry a personage to have a seat side by side
with the Papacy. This arrangement, therefore—the
Pope at Rome, belonging to the King of Italy—is a
dream; it is worse: it is the extreme of ignorance
. . . It is in Rome that the great past, which is called
the Papacy, must abide, and abide alone."

Following these speakers came Moustier, stating the
opinion of his government, that " Italian unity was not
considered by France as bound up with the possession
of Rome.;" and then he added the further sting that " it
must be avowed that upon the side of the Holy See there
are good reasons for being suspicious of Italy."

. In the Legislative Body, true to his principles, Jules

Favre denounced the sending of troops to the defence of
Rome. He was silenced by Thiers in one of the most
successful efforts of indignant oratory made during the
whole debate. "Under cover of French intervention,"
he said, "the weak princes of Italy have been overthrown. Reproaches were not uttered when we inter-
vened for the despoiler, and are they to be launched
against our intervention for the last that has been
robbed? The House of Savoy has hunted with Garibaldi
as its falcon. The situation, I know, is difficult for
France, between Victor Emmanuel, unhappy in his
grandeur at the Pitti Palace, and the Pope, menaced in
the last remaining ruins of the temporal power. How
are we to get out of the difficulty? By an act of frank-
ness. By saying to Italy: 'I have compromised the
most important interests by allowing you to unite with
Prussia. I have left the world to doubt of my loyal
intentions by handing over to you the petty States of
Italy. But there is one thing which I cannot abandon
to you, and that is my honour, by delivering up the
Papacy.'" Last came Rouher, Minister of State, if
possible more contemptuous and more outspoken than
the rest. In a speech, often interrupted by bursts of
applause, he stated the fixed determination of France
that Rome should be Catholic, and not Italian. "In
preserving Rome from invasion," he exclaimed, "we
have saved Italy from anarchy. . . . We declare that
Italy shall not seize upon Rome. France will never
submit to such a violence committed on her honour and
her Catholicity. She demands from Victor Emmanuel
the rigorous execution of the Convention of September,
1864, and if this be not conceded, she will supply the

deficiency herself. Is that clear enough? Italy will
find France on the road to Rome the day on which she
attempts to invade the Pontifical territory; and by Rome
I mean the present actual possessions of the Holy See in
all their integrity. There is not the least equivoque in
our intentions on this subject."

All these were hard words spoken by one ally of the
other; yet if we compare this debate with that in the Italian
Parliament a few days later we shall feel that the French
Government knew exactly the kind of men it had to deal
with, and, being resolved to defend the Pontiff against
those whom fear alone can bind, was quite justified in the
strong language in which it expressed its determination.

Menabrea, the President of the Florence Ministry,
showed in his opening speech what reliance is to be placed
upon the most solemn engagements entered into by his
Government. He said: "Rome, being in an isolated
position in the centre of Italy, prevents freedom of com-
munication between the provinces of the Italian kingdom;
but this difficulty is not to be solved by violence. All
rashness must be avoided, and even the thought of
violence dismissed. . . . . Let us not discuss or even
affirm the principle all have at heart. . . . . We must
not compromise ourselves in any way." Having spoken
for some time in this cowardly and (in the face of recent
events) self-condemning strain, the true Italian policy burst
out at length in undisguised treachery: "*Only let the
French evacuate the Pontifical territory,*" he exclaimed.
"As to what we shall then do with the 'Convention,' we
shall act *as may be in our interest.* . . . . When the
French have left, we may then consider whether it *be our
interest* to confirm our engagements or to annul them, or

to establish others so as best to *guard our interests.*"
After this despicable traitor came Ratazzi, who was not
ashamed to say : " With regard to the 'Roman Question,'
we must be prompt to seize an opportune moment. . . . .
As to Garibaldi's enterprize, the moment was *inopportune*
and the time ill-chosen."

And yet, in the face of language such as the above,
there were to be found statesmen who expressed surprise
that France was not ready to believe the words of Italy
when she declared how great was her desire to preserve
the independence of the Sovereign Pontiff, and how honest
were her intentions in reference to Rome. And such men
asked, when would France evacuate the States of the
Church, and cease to be a menace to Italy ?

•An answer, which was at the same time a defiance, was
given by the French Emperor himself : " The troops of
France will occupy Civita Vecchia until that moment
when the Holy Father shall be no longer threatened by a
single enemy."

Thus the sword of what was then the first army in the
world was pledged to defend " the most ancient, the most
legitimate of all human possessions." How this pledge
came to be violated, and the consequences which have
followed upon this violation, will form part of the second
volume of this work.

PRO PETRI SEDE.

D. Lane, Printer, 310, Strand, London, W.C.

R

Lightning Source UK Ltd.
Milton Keynes UK
UKHW022110080223
416681UK00011B/2703

9 781017 399660